A Jewish Girlhood in Berlin, 1859–1879

A Memoir

To Priscilla + Paula
Tit for tat.
Olga + David
Aug. 2020

A Jewish Girlhood in Berlin, 1859–1879

A Memoir

by Jenny Barth Bornstein

৵ ৽

Translated, edited and annotated by

Olga Bornstein Wise and David Wise

2010

FOR THE DESCENDANTS OF
JENNY BARTH BORNSTEIN (1859–1951)
AND OF HER SISTERS
JOHANNA (1851–1922)
AND PAULA (1867–1942)

TABLE OF CONTENTS

PART I
Introduction   1
Timeline   11
Map and Photographs   13

PART II – A JEWISH GIRLHOOD IN BERLIN
Birth   27
My First Mama – Bella   29
Papa   35
Early Childhood and Relatives   43
Governesses – Age Four   55
Divorce – Bella's Tragedy   65
Papa Remarries   71
My Second Mama – Therese   79
The Lenz School for Girls   85
Family Life   91
1870 – The Exhilaration of Victory   97
The Family Prospers   101
Adolescence, School and Friends   113
Philipp   127
Interlude in Saxony   139
Engaged   147

PART III
Epilogue – Jenny's Later Life and Descendants   153
My Recollections of Jenny, by Olga Wise   161
Additional Photographs and Documents   165
The Memoir's Translators/Editors   175
Bibliography   177

PART I

INTRODUCTION

his work is a memoir by Jenny Barth Bornstein (1859–
1951). Jenny was born, raised and schooled in Berlin;
she married in 1880 and was widowed in 1891; she
raised three children, studied medicine in Switzerland at a time
when German universities were closed to women, and was
licensed as one of the first dozen female physicians in Germany
in 1902. She practiced medicine in Berlin until 1912. In 1935,
two years after the Nazis came to power, Jenny emigrated from
Germany to Palestine and from there to the United States. She
died in Herrin, Illinois at the age of ninety-one. Her memoir,
written in German, covers the years 1859–1879, the years of her
infancy, girlhood and adolescence.

One of the memoir's two translators and editors, Olga
Bornstein Wise, is Jenny's great-granddaughter; she knew Jenny
during her own childhood in Illinois. Jenny's manuscript reached
us on Labor Day 2009, when Olga's Israeli-born cousin Naomi
Wolman brought it from Los Angeles to Austin. Naomi had
learned of the manuscript's existence only a month earlier
through a chance conversation in Tel Aviv, and obtained it from
Margaret Singer, a descendant of Jenny's sister Paula who lives
in England. The memoir thus returned to the United States, where
it was written. For us it was a completely unexpected find. Once
Olga had transcribed the manuscript for easier reading, the

liveliness and detail of her narrative soon convinced us that it deserved translation.

Jenny wrote her memoir in longhand, in a lined American school copybook with a streamlined diesel passenger locomotive pictured on the front. It is plausible that she was spurred to write it by the birth in 1941 of her first two American great-grandchildren, Olga and twin brother Philipp. Jenny wrote the memoir, or most of it, during 1941 in Washington, D.C., at the home of her nephew Erich Fraenkel, where she was then living.

We have translated the manuscript into English, editing it to improve its narrative flow and dividing it into short chapters. We have omitted as little as possible. We have added footnotes where we thought the American reader might be unfamiliar with a historical event, location, person or date, or with a word, phrase or custom. We have also included a small number of photographs and documents. An epilogue offers additional family history and Olga's childhood recollections of Jenny. Finally, we have included a short list of secondary sources for the reader who wishes to know more about the history of the German Jews (especially in the nineteenth century), about women's lives and work during the German Empire, or about the pioneering women physicians of the final decade of the nineteenth century and the early years of the twentieth.

A HISTORICAL MOMENT

Jenny's memoir recounts her early life in an increasingly prosperous middle-class Berlin Jewish household during the 1860s and 1870s. Her narrative gives us a fascinating entry into the world of urban German Jews of these two decades. Some historical context is necessary.

During Jenny's childhood and adolescence, German Jews numbered approximately half a million, or slightly over one percent of the total German population. Two thirds of Germany's Jews lived in Prussia; in its capital city, Berlin, they made up four to five percent of the population.[1] The 1860s and 1870s saw greatly increased Jewish rural–urban migration; in the cities, Jews became middle-class, and in many cases secular. When German unification was realized in 1871, Berlin became the capital of a powerful new empire; its commerce and its population boomed. Berlin's Jews, politically emancipated and with already developed commercial skills, greatly increased their participation in the commercial, civic and political life of the city and of the Empire. Their heightened profile soon brought a reaction; in the 1880s there emerged a political and social anti-Semitism that would later grow in shrillness and strength. That reaction, however, is not foreshadowed in Jenny's memoir.

Viewed in retrospect, the 1860s and the 1870s, the decades immediately preceding and following German unification, were a period of national enthusiasm and optimism, of rising Jewish prosperity and of greatly enhanced prospects for social acceptance and integration. We think we perceive, in the predominantly happy tone of Jenny's memoir, not just the alert curiosity and high spirits of her childhood personality, but also

---

[1] Richarz, Monika, ed., *Jewish Life in Germany: Memoirs from Three Centuries* (Bloomington, Ind., 1991), pp. 5–9, for these statistics.

the general optimism of a relatively happy and prosperous interlude in German–Jewish history.

The household in which Jenny is born and raised is Jewish, German, and middle class.[2] It is in first place Jewish. Almost all the characters in Jenny's memoir are Jewish; the few others are minor. This reflects the social reality of nineteenth-century Germany: Jews and Christians interacted in the workplace and in the school, but the social circles they inhabited rarely intersected. The Jewishness of Jenny's household, however, is in rapid mutation from the traditional Judaism of the countryside and small towns where most German Jews still lived. Although Jenny may write admiringly of the observant piety of her grandfather Landsberger or of her country uncle David Leser, that is not the reality of her home. Her father observes no Jewish traditions; the memoir makes no mention of religious education; Jenny visits the synagogue only on major holidays. In short, the household is becoming secular.[3] Indeed, as German Jews urbanized, acculturated, and sometimes strove to become "more German than the Germans," traditional religious observances often fell away, were de-emphasized or relegated to home use. In many cases, an ethic of work, education and culture (*Bildung*) came to fill the role previously played by religion. At the same time, the

---

[2] "Jewish," "German," and "middle class" are the three concepts fundamental to Marion A. Kaplan's *The Making of the Jewish Middle Class: Women, Family, and Identity in Imperial Germany* (New York, 1991), the single work we found of greatest help in understanding Jenny's German–Jewish world.

[3] Jenny's sister Paula states, in her unpublished memoir, that her mother (Jenny's stepmother) Therese maintained a kosher household. This was a Jewish practice that faded relatively slowly; older relatives, whether members of the household or visitors, needed to be accommodated.

customs and symbols of the larger German society were adopted and displayed. It was thus by no means unusual (to take one example) for middle-class Jewish families to celebrate the Christmas season with a Christmas tree, lights and the giving of gifts, as Jenny recounts in her memoir.

JENNY THE CHILD, JENNY THE AUTHOR

Jenny was an impetuous child of strong likes and dislikes. For practical purposes, she was motherless from 1863, when her father, Israel, divorced her birth mother, Bella, until 1866, when he married her stepmother, Therese. Jenny paints herself as an energetic, curious and strong-willed child, often struggling or rebelling against the rules and expectations of household, school and society. She flatly refuses, for example, to learn to knit or embroider (an obligatory female activity), and gets away with it. As an adolescent, she requires patient mentoring as she learns social graces and self-control. As a young woman of twenty, she rejects out of hand an advantageous offer of marriage from a wealthy suitor because her heart inclines toward Philipp Bornstein. As a narrator, she does not mince words about people she dislikes, and her candor is sometimes startling.

Jenny's memoir is selective, not comprehensive. We must keep in mind that it was written over sixty years after the episodes it relates; there is no guarantee of factual correctness. In addition, memoirs necessarily contain distortions, whether deliberate or inadvertent. They are literary constructions, not diaries or chronicles. Jenny's memoir is indeed literary. Her generation was a highly literate generation. As students, she and her middle-class contemporaries learned the German classics; as adults they devoured countless novels, plays and works of history. From her own reading, her high-school education, and her Uncle Siegmund's literary tutoring, Jenny absorbed a sense for plot, dialogue and dramatic moment that she puts to good use in her memoir.

Jenny's basic literary device is the episode or vignette, which she uses to encapsulate and present the key experiences of her childhood and adolescence, together with the emotions that accompanied them or the lessons she drew from them. The narrative is loosely structured. The story line is generally chronological, but Jenny often loops back to add detail to an event she has already covered. Sometimes she leaps forward dramatically, as in her account of the death of her mother, Bella. She writes an educated but lively and colloquial German, and she makes extensive and effective use of dialogue, perhaps an indication that she envisioned a young audience for her stories.

The first half of the narrative is the stronger. The lively, detail-filled sketches from her childhood years reach a high point in the short gem titled "1870 — The Exhilaration of Victory," in which she relives her experience of Berlin's ecstatic celebration of Prussia's military victory over France in September 1870. The intensity of the narrative then slackens as Jenny turns her attention to relatives in and outside Berlin, to excursions on the Rhine and annual vacations in spa towns, and to the lessons, teachers and friends of her high-school years. Most of the memoir's final quarter is devoted to the year 1879 and to Jenny's courtship by Philipp Bornstein. Despite the obvious strength of Jenny's feelings for her fiancé, the Philipp of the memoir is an idealized and wooden figure, upon whom Jenny projects her hopes and her ideals of romantic and marital love. The memoir ends with a novelistic flourish as Jenny takes her irrevocable decision to marry Philipp.

KEY CHARACTERS

Jenny's memoir (Jenny aside) is peopled by several dozen characters. They include members of her immediate and extended family, wet nurses, governesses, playmates, teachers, schoolmates, servants and finally, a fiancé. Five characters are of particular importance in Jenny's life and development. First is her father, Israel Barth (1824–1892), an ambitious man who immigrated to Berlin from the province of Posen in the 1840s and became established as a textile and clothing merchant. Israel is lovingly sketched. His role in Jenny's early childhood was much more prominent than that normally played by middle-class fathers, due in good part to the fact that he was a single parent to Jenny and Hanne for three years. Jenny recalls in affectionate detail the attention her father lavished on her as a young child.

Second is Jenny's early-married and flighty birth mother, Bella, whose life served Jenny as a powerful cautionary tale. Bella's absence from most of Jenny's childhood is conspicuous. After Israel divorced her, Bella remarried and later moved to Dresden. Her life there was unhappy; she died in squalor in 1880, leaving several orphaned children. Jenny's account of Bella's final illness and death is full of pathos. Her "utterly wasted" life served Jenny as an object lesson and a warning of the seriousness a woman's life choices demanded.

Third is Israel's second wife, Therese Simon-Meyer, who entered Jenny's life when she was six. Therese, an intelligent, perceptive and practical woman, proved a true second mother to

Jenny, and gave her loving and much-needed guidance. Therese came from a poor family and did not let the prosperity of the Barth household dull her conviction that a woman needed a practical education and the capacity to earn money. She saw to it that Jenny obtained, beyond a standard secondary education, a teaching certificate she could rely on in hard times. Above all, she instilled in Jenny an ethic of resolute self-reliance.

Fourth is Jenny's favorite uncle, Therese's brother Siegmund, who tutored Jenny in the German classics when she was between twelve and fourteen. Jenny writes that Uncle Siegmund "should have been a psychologist or an actor;" he was cut out for higher things than the world of commerce he inhabited. Jenny relates that she and Uncle Siegmund would choose parts and read aloud the plays of Lessing, Goethe and Schiller, and then discuss plot and character at length. "Uncle Siegmund did not discourage me from expressing my own ideas. He sometimes took the opposing view, but he did not demand that I agree with him." Uncle Siegmund's contribution to Jenny's intellectual development was to set her on the path of independent and critical thinking.

Last is Jenny's older sister Hanne, who is either present or close at hand throughout the narrative. In Jenny's portrait of Hanne, we note the ambivalent relationship of a younger child to her older sibling. Jenny observes and reports on Hanne's behavior with puzzlement, admiration, envy or (as when Hanne attempts to elope with "a tall blond American") an amazed fascination. Jenny, to a great extent, defined herself in opposition to Hanne, and there is no doubt that the two sisters were strikingly different in temperament and outlook. Hanne, when compared with Jenny, is a party girl; when she finally marries at age twenty-seven, it is because "one has to get married eventually." The following contrast is telling: when Hanne transgresses the family doctor's orders, she does so by dancing; Jenny disobeys his orders by reading Shakespeare.

JENNY'S MEMOIR: A PROLOGUE TO A LIFE

We have spent much of the last year with Jenny's memoir. Our main reason for doing so was selfish; we wanted to satisfy our curiosity about an unusual woman and the society in which she came to adulthood. This curiosity has been only half satisfied. Jenny's memoir provides no sense of finality or summation; it breaks off when she has lived less than a quarter of what will be a very long life. Jenny did not embark on the genuinely pioneering segment of her life, that of her medical studies and her practice as one of Germany's first female physicians, until the age of thirty-three, and she lived for forty years after she abandoned her medical career in 1912. We would be selling Jenny's narrative short to say that it ends "just as it was starting to get interesting," but it is in fact only an introduction to a life filled with upheavals, accomplishments, and tragedy. Although we wish we could follow Jenny farther into adulthood, we must take leave of her as she prepares for marriage at age twenty.

Jenny's Life – a Timeline

1824	Jenny's father, Israel Barth, born in Prussian province of Posen.
1840s	Israel migrates to Berlin, enters clothing/textiles business.
1848	Liberal, pro-democratic protests and rebellions against the old political order break out through Western Europe, including the German states.
1850	Israel marries Bella Landsberger.
1851	Jenny's older sister Johanna (Hanne) born.
1859	Jenny born.
1862	Otto von Bismarck becomes Minister-President of Prussia, pursues politics of German unification under Prussian leadership.
1863	Israel divorces Bella; Hanne and Jenny under care of governesses.
1864	Prussia defeats Denmark in short war, annexes territory.
1866	Prussia defeats Austria, assumes leadership of German Confederation; Israel marries Therese Simon-Meyer; Jenny begins elementary school.
1867	Jenny's younger sister Paula born.
1870	Prussia defeats France, becomes Europe's leading military power.
1871	Unified German Empire created with Berlin as capital; complete legal emancipation for Jews (occupational and social discrimination persisted); boom in industry and housing.
1871–73	Jenny's family prospers; Israel invests in real estate; Jenny continues her schooling; family travels within Germany.

1875–76	Jenny finishes secondary school; earns teaching certificate.
1879	Jenny meets and becomes engaged to Israel's associate Philipp Bornstein.
1880	Jenny marries Philipp; Hanne marries Israel's associate Wilhelm Bütow; Bella dies.
1881–88	Therese dies (1881); Jenny gives birth to three children (Arthur, Therese/Rose, and Suzanne).
1891–92	Philipp dies (December 1891); Israel dies (March 1892).
1893	Jenny moves with her children to Switzerland, enters medical school in Zürich.
1898	Jenny receives her Swiss medical degree; returns to Berlin; employed as in-house doctor for merchant and trade association.
1902	Jenny licensed as one of first dozen female physicians in Germany.
1902–12	Jenny practices medicine in Berlin (obstetrics and gynecology).
1912	Jenny abandons medicine, moves to Hamburg to manage household of her widowed son Arthur and to help raise grandson Frederick.
1935	Jenny leaves Germany for Palestine.
1937	Jenny immigrates to the United States.
1941	Jenny's first American great-grandchildren (Olga and Philipp) born; Jenny writes her memoir.
1951	Jenny dies and is buried in Herrin, Illinois.

MAP and PHOTOGRAPHS

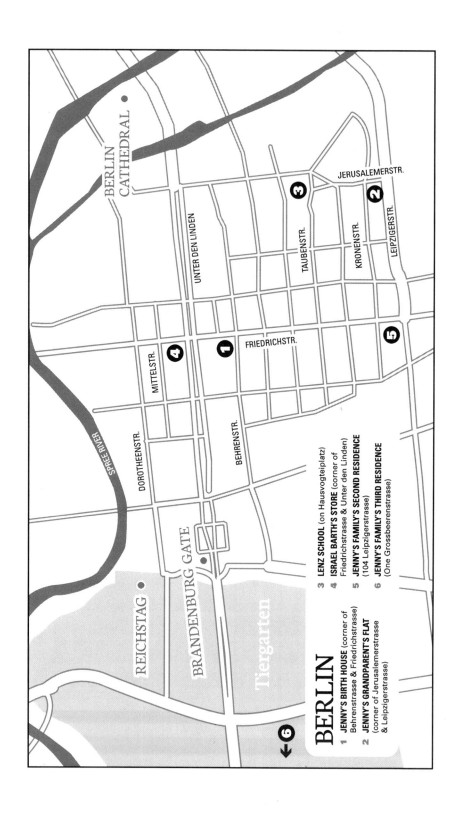

BERLIN

1 **JENNY'S BIRTH HOUSE** (corner of Behrenstrasse & Friedrichstrasse)
2 **JENNY'S GRANDPARENT'S FLAT** (corner of Jerusalemerstrasse & Leipzigerstrasse)
3 **LENZ SCHOOL** (on Hausvogteiplatz)
4 **ISRAEL BARTH'S STORE** (corner of Friedrichstrasse & Unter den Linden)
5 **JENNY'S FAMILY'S SECOND RESIDENCE** (104 Leipzigerstrasse)
6 **JENNY'S FAMILY'S THIRD RESIDENCE** (One Grossbeerenstrasse)

Fig. 1 (facing page). Map of Berlin in the mid-nineteenth century
Fig. 2 (this page). Cover of notebook in which Jenny wrote
her memoir

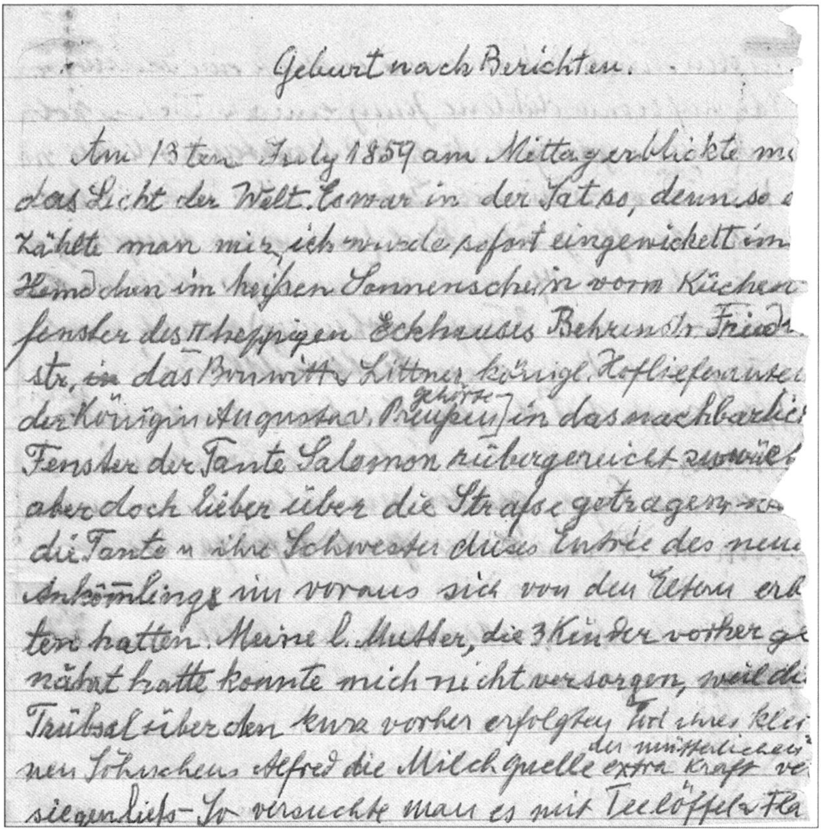
Geburt nach Berichten.

Am 13ten July 1859 am Mittag erblickte m
das Licht der Welt. Es war in der Tat so, denn so e
zählte man mir, ich wurde sofort eingewickelt im
Hemdchen im heißen Sonnenschein vorm Küchen-
fenster des II treppigen Eckhauses Behrenstr. Fried
str., ~~in~~ das Bruwitt u. Littner königl. Hoflieferanten
der Königin Augusta v. Preußen gehörte in das nachbarlic
Fenster der Tante Salomon rübergereicht zuweil
aber doch lieber über die Straße getragen, wo
die Tante u. ihre Schwester dieses Entrée des neu
Ankömmlings im voraus sich von den Eltern erb
ten hatten. Meine l. Mutter, die 3 Kinder vorher ge
nährt hatte konnte mich nicht versorgen, weil di
Trübsal über den kurz vorher erfolgten Tod ihres klei
nen Söhnchens Alfred die Milchquelle der mütterlichen extra Kraft ve
siegen ließ. So versuchte man es mit Teelöffel u. Fla

Fig. 3. First page of Jenny's handwritten memoir

Fig. 4. Israel Barth (1824–1892)

Fig. 5. Jenny (on chair) at about age two, with sister Hanne

Fig. 6. Therese Simon-Meyer Barth (1837–1881)

Fig. 7. Barth family house at Grossbeerenstrasse 1, Berlin

Fig. 8. Jenny and Paula, circa 1872

Fig. 9. Hanne, in her twenties

Fig. 10. Jenny at twenty-one, in 1880

PART II

A JEWISH GIRLHOOD IN BERLIN, 1859–1879

A MEMOIR

BY JENNY BARTH BORNSTEIN

Birth

I first saw the light of day on July 13, 1859. I was told that I was immediately wrapped up in a little baby dress that had been warmed in the sunshine of the kitchen window of the flat across the street from us, where Aunt Solomon[4] lived. The window and Aunt Solomon's apartment were located on the second floor of the two-story house on the corner of Behrenstrasse and Friedrichstrasse[5] that was owned by Queen Auguste of Prussia. This little dress could easily have been handed from the window of her flat to ours, but was instead walked across the street by Aunt Solomon and her sister, who had already asked my parents if they could witness the debut of the new arrival.

My dear mother,[6] who had already nursed three children, could not nurse me because her sorrow over the recent death of her baby son Alfred had dried up her milk. They tried to feed me with a teaspoon and a bottle, but that also failed. I would start to cry as soon they put the spoon in my mouth. After days of fruitless attempts to feed me, the doctor finally looked in my

---

[4] Aunt Solomon and her sister Aunt Bley appear to be relatives of Jenny's mother, Bella Landsberger.

[5] A major intersection in central Berlin, only blocks from the Brandenburg Gate.

[6] Bella (Bertha) Barth née Landsberger (1833?–1880)

mouth and saw that it was grayish-green in color. After this, little Jenny got a healthy Polish wet nurse and began to thrive. After eight or nine months, however, my dear Father discovered that this fine Giver of All Good Things was sneaking out of the house and over the roof at night (we had recently moved to 24 Behrenstrasse, where there was a low annex to the three-story house). He immediately dismissed the night-wandering wet nurse. "And what?" said the Polish woman, "So now this child, with her tender little bones, is supposed to drink cow's milk?" Father[7] would tell me this later whenever the subject came up. But I am grateful to her. Her milk must have been very good.

---

[7] Israel Barth (1824–1892), who came to Berlin in the 1840s from Posen, a mainly Polish-speaking province of Prussia.

My First Mama – Bella

I remember little about the first three years of my life. Now and then my mother's face appears. Five or six things stick in my memory. My mother is standing in front of the tiled stove. A cook pot, which seemed gigantic to me, is full of steaming meat broth. Mama fills six or eight bowls with it, puts a bit of soup meat and potatoes in them, and opens the kitchen door that gives directly onto the front steps, where poorly dressed women are standing, some with children and some without. She gives each of them a bowl of soup and some bread. I cannot hear what they are saying. Their shabby clothing strikes my eye and makes me wonder. Why does it look so grey? The children's clothes too? Why don't their mothers feed them and sew for them the way our mother does? I don't understand it. The women came almost every day. I saw this scene often, and still can't get it out of my mind.

Mama knitted many fine things for me and my older sister, Hanne,[8] including petticoats and underwear of the finest batiste. Hanne would sometimes run out onto the Kissinger Promenade without a dress, to the amazement of the high-class public there. In addition, Mama produced an amazing number of tapestry-

---

[8] The given name of Jenny's older sister (born 1851) is Johanna = Hanna or Hanne = Hannchen (diminutive). For the sake of consistency, we have opted for "Hanne."

work items: gloves, little mats and pillowcases. These items did not stay in the house; Mama took them with her when she went out. And I began to realize that Papa couldn't stand these things. As soon as his familiar steps were heard on the stairs, Mama would throw her work and the wool into a brown cabinet and lock it up.

When I was much, much older, twenty or twenty-one, I realized why she had done all this needlework — it wasn't for us or the household. Papa provided amply for Mama's needs, and Uncle Julius[9] brought her beautiful dresses from Paris every new fashion season. What did she do with this money she earned in secret? Did she have her own private bank account? At the age of three and a half, however, I didn't give a second thought to Mama's work, to the fact that one can earn money by working, or even that it was necessary to earn money.

I was not as happy when Mama took me out with her, because that meant going to Aunt Labanter's[10] house. That was a trial of patience for me, because I had to sit completely still in the room, on a long piece of furniture about two feet off the floor, and completely quiet, while Aunt Labanter talked with Mama; the two often left the room. There was no aunty friendliness, no toys, no playing, nothing to eat, and not a word spoken to me.

We would also go out every week or two down the old Schoenehaus Promenade to the cemetery. The ride in the horse-drawn tram was nice, but then we would visit the grave of

---

[9] Julius Landsberger, one of Bella's brothers.
[10] Unknown relative.

Mama's mother, Hanna Landsberger.[11] I never knew her because she died twelve years before I was born. Mama would throw herself on the grave and cry, the grave that she lovingly planted with ivy and flowers, mostly hydrangeas (which for that reason I never liked having in my room). She wept inconsolably for what seemed like hours, talking to the dead. I realized this from her words, but I didn't understand the rest of it. Then she would visit the two little graves of my older siblings who had died. I had no way to share Mama's grief. For me death was only a word, not a concept.

I was equally indifferent when Mama played the piano. While I loved to hear Papa singing in the morning, as well as the violin playing of Aunt Bley's eighteen-year-old foster son (who became Concertmaster Rehfeld[12] at the Royal Berlin Opera House), I did not enjoy listening to Mama's two favorite pieces, "The Maiden's Prayer"[13] and "Invitation to the Dance."[14] When she played, I had to sit completely quiet. Sitting quietly was not the problem, because when Papa sang I listened raptly with full attention, and likewise when the violin played. Only now and then would I tell the virtuoso disapprovingly, "Fabian, you hit another wrong note." He would come over laughing to me and say, "You heard that? Someday you'll be my bride!" How I, at three and a half, enjoyed that! I don't know which I enjoyed more, the words

---

[11] Hanna (Johanna) Landsberger (died 1847). Jenny's sister Hanne was likely named after her.

[12] Fabian Rehfeld (1842–1920), Berlin violinist, conductor and composer.

[13] A popular musical piece in the second half of the nineteenth century, by Polish composer Tekla Badarzewska (1834–1861).

[14] Originally an orchestral piece by composer Carl Maria von Weber (1786–1826).

"Someday you'll be my bride," or the fact that I had caught his wrong note and teased him about it. Perhaps both.

I remember a wonderful summer day. My Uncle and Aunt Jonas Speyer[15] came and picked up my parents, Hanne and me to go a concert at Kroll's[16] in the Tiergarten.[17] The street was bright with sunshine; my mother was walking between Uncle and Aunt Speyer, with Papa and us children behind the three of them. I couldn't take my eyes off my mother. The sun shone golden on her hair, which her little Parisian "forget-me-not" hat left uncovered, and her simple but stylish dress (brought by Uncle Julius) enfolded her like a princess from Wonderland. I was lost in amazement and forgot everything else. I started to skip. My sister noticed it and shouted, "Papa, she's doing it again, she always does it as soon as she's out of the house!" Papa didn't say anything, but a bit farther along he turned around and told me, "Go and run, but come back soon." I wonder if he too had been daydreaming about the princess from Wonderland. Then we all walked on through the Tiergarten to Kroll's, where we had a fine time.

One morning I watched Mama as she was taking things out of cupboards and closets and packing them into boxes and suitcases. I wasn't paying a lot of attention, but I was surprised when she took from the buffet a tea service whose golden shine had always

---

[15] Jonas Speyer was a relative (possibly a brother) of Jenny's deceased grandmother.

[16] Kroll's Etablissement in the Tiergarten, founded in 1844, was a so-called *café chantant*. It consisted of a large coffee house with a variety theater (the *Krolloper*) attached.

[17] The Tiergarten ("animal park") is an enormous park in Berlin; it was originally the king's hunting park.

fascinated me. I cried, "Mama, why are you packing up the tea service?"

"I'm taking it with me because it belongs to me," was her answer.[18] I didn't understand. Mama had gone on trips with Uncle Julius before, but she had never taken the tea service with her. I sat there unhappily, as if anesthetized, and didn't ask any more questions.

Mama went away shortly after this. Then my first governess, a big fat homely older woman who dressed in gray, moved in with us. She slept in Mama's bed, I slept in the same room next to the window, and Hanne slept in Papa's bed. This was all very puzzling to me. Hanne wouldn't tell me anything, and nobody spoke about Mama again until years later.

---

[18] A bride often brought items such as a tea service into a marriage as part of her trousseau.

PAPA

This is how I usually spent my days when I was between three and six. Early in the morning, about seven or half past, Papa would come into the bedroom I shared with Hanne. This room, which we called the Alcove, was next to our parents' bedroom. He would sit down on my bed and say, "Look what the cat brought you during the night." I would search under my pillow, and every morning — even in summer — I would find a big brown gingerbread cookie. Papa would bring me a wine glass full of water, and I would have to drink it while I ate the gingerbread. Then he would stand in front of the big dressing-table mirror and comb and brush his hair for what seemed like an hour. This wasn't boring to me, however, because he would sing the whole time in his warm voice: folk songs, arias, children's songs, and occasionally student and military songs. I learned the melodies, of course, but I didn't sing along with him. Instead I listened to him entranced. His full clear voice, from the low notes to the high, so enchanted me that I sat silent and still in bed. Then, with me still in my nightgown, we would have breakfast in the "Berlin Room." Mama and I would sit on the green plush sofa,[19] Papa to my right on a high plush chair. Hanne was probably already in school, because I don't know where she sat.

---

[19] This is obviously before Bella's departure from the household.

After Papa had gone to his store, right after breakfast, I was dressed and then immediately ran to the Konströms (they were Swedish). They lived on the floor below ours and had ten children. What the older children did, I don't know. Hanne was friends with Minchen and Clara, who were about fifteen and thirteen, respectively. I would play with Paul and Max, who were nine and seven, and played mother to Alex, who was about three, and to Cielchen (Cecilia) who was two. When I got there in the morning, I was allowed to wash both children, dress them and comb their hair. Cielchen was the one who interested me most. First, her head was covered with thick red curls, and I could do all kinds of things to it with hair bands and combs. Second, she seemed very odd to me, because I couldn't figure out whether she was a little girl or a little boy. (Only later, when I was studying medicine, did I realize that I had mistaken her bellybutton for a second urethra.) Frau Konström had no household help, so she let me stay with the children for two or three hours.

When the weather was good, I would run to the Great Courtyard and watch stage props being made at Gichler's in the castle theater. Then I would go into the stables, where the horses Hans and Liese were sometimes already waiting for me to bring them lumps of sugar or turnips. Because I was so little, most of these fell on the ground, but the horses usually found them anyway. Finally Paul and Max would get out of school and we would play in the courtyard warehouse of the Schleip Company, which owned the building we lived in, on the piles of beautiful fresh-cut boards they used in making pianos. We would climb around on the boards, jump down off them, throw balls, or lay a board on top of a wooden block to make a seesaw. Then we would play hide-and-seek with Hanne, "One, two, three — here I come!"[20] Sometimes children would come out of the neighboring houses, and we would play circle games or war. At half past one we stopped for lunch.

Also in good weather, our servant Carl[21] would pick me up around half past three or half past four and take me to Papa's store. Then Papa and I would walk through the Tiergarten for two hours or more. That was the high point of my day. From Kranzler's,[22] an elegant coffee and pastry store on the corner of Friedrichstrasse and Unter den Linden,[23] we would walk through the Linden Promenade. Most of the benches on both sides of this broad promenade were occupied by children and grownups. A sixpence would drop into my hand; "Jenny, run over to the court bakery and get yourself a croissant." I would cross the riding path (there were riding paths on both sides of the promenade all the way from the Castle[24] to the Brandenburg Gate[25]) and come back with a delicious croissant. If there was an unoccupied bench, I

---

[20] *"Wer am besten rennt kommt vorbei,"* in the original.

[21] Carl was a house servant; he may also have had duties at Israel's store.

[22] Café Kranzler was established in 1835, and has been part of Berlin's social life ever since.

[23] Unter den Linden ("Under the Linden Trees") was a tree-shaded path built in the seventeenth century to connect the king's castle to his hunting park (Tiergarten). It developed into Berlin's main boulevard.

[24] Castle (City Palace): home of the Prussian kings and later the kaisers. Constructed in the eighteenth century. Demolished in the 1950s by the East German government to build the East German Parliament (now likewise demolished).

[25] Unter den Linden leads to the Brandenburg Gate (constructed 1788–1791), one of the city gates providing entry into Berlin. The Gate is the universally-recognized emblem of Berlin and one of the most famous landmarks in Europe.

would jump on and off it until Papa came and got me. We would continue in this fashion up to the Pariser Platz,[26] where we stopped in front of the sentry house on the parade grounds. Sometimes one of the king's or the princess's carriages would come through the Brandenburg Gate, and then we would hear, "Present arms!" The company of soldiers saluted, music played, the people took of their hats and waved. Oh, what fun to be a child again!

Papa, smiling, would march with me through the gate, cut across the square in front of the Tiergarten, and turn into the Lion Promenade. Two hundred paces further on we came to an old crippled soldier standing on his one leg and cranking his hurdy-gurdy. The only tune this street organ ever played was the "Entry into Paris" march. At his side stood his poor wife, dressed shabbily in a worn-out soldier's coat and cap and holding out her hand. I would take Papa's sixpence and throw it into the little box or put it in the woman's outstretched hand.

Continuing our walk, we came next to the goldfish pond, where Papa would let me sit on a bench and eat my croissant while he stood leaning on his ivory-handled cane. The goldfish got a pinch of my croissant along with the crumbs. Now the path became narrower and deserted until it reached Rousseau Island.[27] There Papa would start to declaim, usually singing or reciting Uhland's poems[28] or freedom songs. When he found a pretty

---

[26] Pariser Platz (Paris Square) fronts the Brandenburg Gate.

[27] Rousseau Island, in the Tiergarten, was named for the French philosopher and novelist Rousseau, who advocated a return to nature.

[28] Romantic poet Ludwig Uhland (1787–1862) is remembered for his ballads and patriotic verse.

little wildflower growing in the grass, he would point to it with his cane, which meant, "You can go ahead and pick it," and tell me its name. Seventy-eight years ago one could still walk on the grass in the Tiergarten! We made our way through the Tiergarten up to Rousseau Island, and from there we clambered through the trees and bushes up to the new lake. If there were riders gathered at the Hippodrome,[29] Papa would stop there for a long time. Each horse would be praised, admired or criticized, and the reasons explained to me. Papa had a great love for good, beautiful horses. Even when he took a horse-drawn taxi,[30] he would look and look until he found the cab whose horse he liked best. Then we would walk across the Seyzen Promenade with its old, thick trees and rest a little while at the Schneckenberg.[31] From there we would take home the flowers I had picked. "*Allons*, to Mother," he would cry.

Papa also had a different walking route that went through the tents.[32] There he let me buy us each a cinnamon cookie for two three-penny coins from the baker woman who stood in front of Tent Number II. Then we would walk back to Bellevue Castle[33]

---

[29] Racetrack, no longer in existence.

[30] Here Jenny uses the word "*droschke.*" A droschke (the word is Russian) was a versatile horse-drawn carriage. It could be pulled by a single horse, and was often used as a taxi.

[31] A Schneckenberg (literally, "Snail Mountain") is an artificial hill set in a landscaped garden or park. A spiral path leads to the top.

[32] One section of the Tiergarten contained large tents that were available for summer rental by middle-class Berliners. The predecessors of these tents were set up to house Huguenot (protestant) refugees from France in the mid-eighteenth century.

[33] Bellevue Castle, built 1786, was the residence of the Prussian crown prince. It is now the official residence of the president of Germany.

across the Moabit Meadow[34] with its flowers, water, and rowboats big and small, with Papa telling me "once upon a time" stories. Then we would continue down the Charlottenburger Chaussée[35] to the Brandenburg Gate, and from there back home, sometimes making a detour to stop in at Papa's store.[36]

This was the time of day that the Landtag deputies[37] and the ambassadors would be placing their orders or coming in for a fitting. Papa's brother Uncle Emmanuel[38] would show the fabrics and the tailor would take measurements,[39] nearly everything taking place without the customers even saying yes or no; they simply followed Papa's advice. I never heard arguments about price or about anything else. Papa and the sales clerks talked about things that were incomprehensible to me, and if Lasker[40] came in and I was there, he would put his hand on my head and stroke my hair. But I pulled away from him and went to look at

---

[34] Moabit was an industrial suburb adjoining the Tiergarten that was incorporated into Berlin in 1861. It became famous for its teaching hospital and notorious for its prison. Moabit is now an inner-city neighborhood.

[35] The Charlottenburger Chaussée (road) ran from Charlottenburg Castle to the Brandenburg Gate.

[36] Israel's business was located at the intersection of Friedrichstrasse and Unter den Linden.

[37] The Landtag was the Prussian parliament.

[38] Emmanuel Barth (1839–1890?) was an older brother of Israel Barth.

[39] Israel Barth, at this time, is the proprietor of a successful textile and clothing business. Hence the presence of a tailor at the store.

[40] Eduard Lasker (1829–1884), politician and leader of the National Liberal Party. Born in Posen, son of a Jewish tradesman, member of the Prussian House of Representatives (Landtag) 1867–1879. The Liberal Party strongly supported German unification, and was an ally of Bismarck in his early years as Prussian *Ministerpräsident* and then as German chancellor.

the display of the horse bridles that the store made out of bright-colored fabric remnants.

After dinner, Papa would play with us after he had finished the newspaper. He cut dolls and carts and sleighs out of cardboard or made little drawings of chimneysweeps, houses, horses, storks, peacocks and all kinds of animals, using his half-burned matches to sketch with. Eventually he would whistle the military tattoo or sing "Good night, comrade, good night, comrade — sleep well."[41] Sometimes he would give me a big wet loud kiss on the cheek, which I immediately wiped off. He would laugh, and I was later told that I fell asleep singing.

---

[41] The editors have not been able to identify the nineteenth-century song in question.

EARLY CHILDHOOD
AND RELATIVES

I would get up singing the next morning too. However, if there was rain or snow or ice, the day's program would be different. I still did my nanny's job at the Konströms. But there would be no courtyard, street or Tiergarten. Instead there was Aunt Solomon and her kindly sister Aunt Bley with her foster son Fabian Rehfeld the violinist. What a beautiful new world I found there!

Poor Aunt Bley. I always found her in bed. I never saw her any other way, so I didn't really think about it. Aunt Bley and her bed; the two things were all one to me, they went together. I would sit next to the bed on a tall footstool and give her my hand, which she would hold in hers. After we had asked each other a few questions, I would beg her, "Please, Auntie, tell me a story." And then she would start to bring old fairy tales up right before my eyes, as if on a stage. It was better than my story book; Aunt Bley knew how to bring the stories to life and to give her voice the right intonation for every character and situation. That was magical to me; I found myself living right in the midst of these ancient sagas and folk tales. Sometimes Aunt Solomon would come in and tell me it was time to go home for lunch. I realize now that her intention was probably to give her sister some rest. Often Fabian would come in and ask me if I wanted to hear "something new." Of course I did! Once my aunt gave me a big bag of sweets that Aunt Bley had put together for me. The Barths' servant girl came to take me home to eat. When I brought the bag of sweets into the house, Hanne looked through it, took at least half of them out, and said, "Aunt Bley collected this stuff under her pillow. Pfui! You can't eat that — you'll throw up!" And then she walked away with the "nasty stuff."

Sometimes in the early afternoon I would visit the milliner who lived opposite us on the fourth floor. She let me rummage around in her unusable hats, hatbands, veils and so forth, and she decorated and gave me an old hat shell that I had rescued. The following day I didn't find the hat pretty anymore, so I reworked it at least ten times without ever finishing it. But at least this made a rainy day go better.

If the snow outside was dry, I and the other children would make snowmen and throw snowballs, and if there was ice on the ground, we would build a slide path. Sometimes Hanne would go down with me to the candy store in the basement "to find something." Often the store was crowded and we would have to wait. Strangers would ask Hanne if I was her little sister, and she would answer, "Yes," or sometimes, "Maybe." The candy store owner would call out, "Sing, Jenny Lind, sing," and Hanne would turn round and sing Jenny Lind's "Farewell Song," which she knew by heart.[42] (I heard the song again on the radio, two months ago, on March 19, 1941, when a Jenny Lind anniversary was

---

[42] Swedish-born Jenny Lind (1820–1887) was the best-known female opera singer of the nineteenth century. During the 1840s she performed frequently in Germany and became a star in London. She made an extensive concert tour of the United States (1850–1852), promoted by P. T. Barnum.

being celebrated.) I still know that song today. And then a true Berlin miracle happened — the storekeeper was so delighted that he gave me a bag full of his special candy (half chocolate and half nougat). So that I wouldn't gobble it all up, Hanne carried it home and divided it herself.

Before I stop writing about my first four years of life, I need to recall two other little events that are still vivid in my memory. First, two and a half years after Mama had gone away, I was told that Papa was bringing us a second mother, and that I needed to have my first photograph taken (Lucie Koebbel[43] later asked me for it). I was about three and a half, perhaps just four years old. Before the photography session I was told, "You have to be good and stand really still, or the gentleman won't be able to take a picture of you and Hannchen." So I stood like a good child on the little round chair, with Hanne beside me, slender as the number "1." The man behind the covered box told me in a friendly voice to fix my eyes on a certain spot and not to move. I did as I was told, but when I saw movement behind the camera cloth, it flashed into my mind that my new pantaloons, splendid with Mama's needlework, which I was wearing for the first time, ought to be in the picture too. I quickly lifted my dress and petticoats up high so that I and my pantaloons could be photographed! And so they were — thus eternalized for my older and my younger sisters, and for all our neighbors!

The following Sunday morning in bright sunlight Hanne and I walked in complete harmony (a rare occurrence) to the courtyard

---

[43] Lucie Koebbel (née Bütow), Hanne's daughter. Lucie became a physician with the encouragement of her aunt Jenny.

of the building at 19 Behrenstrasse where Zotzmanns' children lived on the second floor. "Zotzmanns!" we yelled several times at the top of our lungs. Finally the two girls peeked out of the window and said, "What do you want?"

We shouted, "Have you had your picture taken yet?"

They replied, "No, Mother says that we have to pay off our debts first."

Hanne and I stood there motionless. The girls didn't say anything else, but I wondered for hours afterward what "debts" might be. When I later asked Hanne what debts were, she replied, "Well, if you go to the candy store and get something and you don't pay for it, that's a debt." I still didn't understand.

The second event is the first Christmas gift-giving that I am able to remember. My parents, Hanne and I were at my grandparents' house. The kitchen was shimmering. It had a glass half-door dividing it from the next room, where bright lights were burning. If Hanne had lifted me up a little, I could have looked through the glass door into the room, but the kitchen servants wouldn't let her. We waited and waited, until finally Papa came and let us in. Lights were burning brightly all around the room, there was a Christmas tree (Grandfather's Jewish faith notwithstanding), and from Grandmother I got a wonderful, beautiful doll with a wax head and light blond hair in a long white batiste needlework dress with blue bows (Arthur[44] wore it when he was a year old). The needlework was Grandmother's. The doll was as big as a one year old baby; I couldn't even carry

---

[44] Arthur Bornstein (1881–1932), Jenny's first child. Arthur became a well-known physician, researcher and professor in Hamburg.

it by myself. (Arthur later played with it when he was a small child, and that was the end of it.) Hanne got one too; it was dressed in red silk with gray ribbons; the Bütow children[45] later played with it.

At that time, if we stayed at my grandparents' house until evening, Hanne and I would spend the night there. We would sleep in Grandma's bed, one of us on each side of her. As soon as I woke up, I would beg her to tell a story. Grandmother would tease us and make us beg her a long time. "All right, what story should I tell?"

"Oh, tell us 'All My Horses, Heeyah!'" That was a wonderful story, and it was true (I recently saw it referred to in a book). Grandmother would tell the story, naming each stop the mail coach made, all the passengers, big and small, what they ate, drank and sang, how often the post horn was blown, what tune it blew, how the coach and its four horses set out from her home town of Salzwedel[46] and two hours later entered a dark, thick forest (this was scary to me), how the robbers sprang out of the forest and tried to seize the coach, how the coachman turned around with his whip, how everyone shrieked in terror, with the coach window broken in, glass flying, blood flowing, etc. How the coachman stood up on his perch, looked around, pulled the reins tight, cracked the whip and cried in a thunderous voice, "All my horses, Heeyah!" Then the horses reared up on their hind legs, the robbers were thrown to the ground and trampled, and the

---

[45] Jenny's sister Hanne married Wilhelm Bütow (1846–1926), a business associate of Israel Barth.

[46] Salzwedel is a town in Saxony-Anhalt, halfway between Hamburg and Magdeburg.

coach drove out of the forest onto the high road and sped back to Salzwedel in a bare half hour. "And if they haven't died by now, they — at least the horses — are still alive today."

After I turned four years old, we no longer spent the night at our grandparents' house,[47] but Hanne and I visited them at least once or twice a week. Grandfather[48] was especially glad to see me. When I went to school, I would stay for lunch with them if I had class in the afternoon, and I liked to visit them in the evening on Friday and on Jewish holidays such as Yom Kippur[49] because of the rituals, the prayers, the candles and the delicious food. By lifting up a stone trapdoor one could climb down from the living room into their dress store,[50] where Grandmother's great-niece Polack and I would play with dolls and crockery and sing. Grandfather would hum along. He was a lovely calm old man who never got angry, but occasionally he would make a mischievous face and wag his finger: "Oh oh, now when Grandmother sees that!"

When I was fifteen or twenty I spent two thirds of a Yom Kippur holiday with my grandparents. I met them in the "Old

---

[47] By the time Jenny was four (in 1863), Israel and Bella were divorced.

[48] In Jenny's memoir, "Grandfather" always refers to Grandfather Landsberger (first name not known, died 1879), the father of her mother, Bella.

[49] Yom Kippur, often called the Day of Atonement, is the Jewish holiday that closes the ten-day period of self-examination and repentance opened by Rosh Hashanah (New Year). The day is observed with synagogue services and fasting. The end of the fast at sundown is usually celebrated with dinner.

[50] Small proprietors commonly had their shop or store on the ground level of a building, and lived with their families above it on the next or "first" floor.

Temple," the synagogue of the very pious.[51] I was glad when the shofar[52] blew and Grandpa picked us up in his droschke. I had fasted along with them, because this was something that made Grandfather happy. We "broke the fast" at their house and had dinner later. Hanne made a short visit to the temple around noon and then came home to break the fast. Mama fasted, but Papa didn't. Nor did Papa go to the temple like Mama did, as long as her health permitted.

Later my little sister Paula was also our grandparents' guest at lunchtime if she had class in the afternoon. They welcomed her with almost more love and attention than they did me, especially Grandfather, who held my stepmother in high regard. When he had occasion to meet her at our flat, he was gentleman and admirer all in one. He greatly respected this woman who loved his grandchildren and brought them up so maternally, and was deeply grateful to her.

When my sister Hanne was fourteen or fifteen, she was given up for dead by our family doctor and medical authority, Doctor Friedrich. She lay in bed with rheumatic fever, unable to move, every movement of the sheets making her cry out in pain. Not even a bath to try to break her high fever seemed to help. Grandfather went to the Old Synagogue in Heidereutergasse. Afterwards he came to our house. I can still see it today. He ran up to my mother, embraced her, and said, "Please don't cry any

---

[51] The "Old Temple" (Old Synagogue) in Berlin was located on Heidereutergasse. Built around 1714, it was destroyed in World War II.

[52] A shofar is a horn, traditionally a ram's horn, used in certain Jewish services. The shofar is blown during the synagogue services for Rosh Hashanah (New Year) and Yom Kippur (Day of Atonement).

more, Frau Barth. Hannchen will get well. I've had her given a new name; her name is Rebecca.[53] And we've prayed for her." This was in the evening. During the night Hanne's fever broke, and by morning her temperature had sunk.

I tell this story to show Grandfather's deep inward piety and the strength of his beliefs. However, he was free of all intolerance, and paid no attention to other people's religion. He placed complete trust in his store clerk/purchaser even though I, at thirteen, could clearly see that he was being deceived. I never heard Grandfather Landsberger say a word about religion, whether Jewish or Catholic. He himself kept all the commandments, but quietly and for his own sake. He disliked excessive talking, even when relatives came to visit. I often saw him quietly leave the room if there was too much talking and "blathering." On the street he often got curious looks from young and old. I remember that even when he was over seventy he would be stared at in the Leipzigerstrasse or in Schöneberg Park[54] when he went out for a summer evening's stroll with Grandma, Hanne and me. The ladies in the park would nudge each other and smile. Grandmother would say, "Landsberger, you must have given her (or them) a sweet look." How Hanne and I would laugh! Then Grandmother would go on and say, "He thinks he was always as handsome as he is now. Age becomes him so!" Hanne and I would giggle to ourselves.

My grandparents' flat had two big attractions. First, it was situated on the corner of Jerusalemerstrasse and Leipzigerstrasse,

---

[53] Presumably so that Death, looking for Hanne under her "old" name, would not be able to find her.

[54] Schöneberg Park is in the Tempelhof district of Berlin.

across from the Dönhoffplatz[55] and the Steinmetz Memorial,[56] so that one could look down from its little balcony in four directions. Weekly markets were held on the square, as was the Little Christmas Market (the big one was around behind the castle in the Breitenstrasse), and there were people's parades with torches, flags, trumpets and drums, for example to celebrate the fall of Sedan,[57] the kaiser's birthday, and so on. Hanne and I would go to their flat to watch the parades along with other family members and friends. There was often quite a crowd, with food for the guests and games for the children.

The other attraction was the neighborhood's street life, which was almost livelier than in Friedrichstrasse. On one side was Steidel's pastry shop, where our Uncle Jonas Speyer often sent us, and on the other side were the colonnade of the Spittelmarkt[58] and Uncle Louis's store.[59] I always needed colored tissue papers, notebooks and coin purses, and I could beg these from Uncle Louis there. So it was always fun for me to spend half a day or the entire day at my grandparents'.

My grandmother was Grandfather Landsberger's second wife. From his first marriage to Hanna (née Speyer), who died young, he had three sons, Bezalie, Julius and Siegmund, and my mother,

---

[55] A square in central Berlin, named for an eighteenth-century garrison commander.

[56] Memorial to Prussian general Karl Friedrich von Steinmetz (1796–1877).

[57] Sedan (September 1, 1870) was the decisive battle in the war against France, which made Prussia into central Europe's dominant military power. "Sedan Day" (September 2) was made an Imperial holiday in 1871.

[58] The Spittelmarkt owes its name to a famous hospital (*Spittel*) that was located on the square.

[59] Uncle Louis was a brother of Israel Barth.

Bella. Only the youngest son, Siegmund, was glad when his father married a second time; the older two continued to mourn for their mother. That was also the reason that Bella, aged barely sixteen, got married as if she were still a child at play. She would put her love letters under her little dog's collar and have the dog carry them to my father. He, at twenty-six, fell in love with his boss's daughter, went out into business on his own, and then married her.[60]

Bella's brothers also left their father's house early. Bezalie went to Copenhagen but later got married in Berlin; Julius spent most of his time in Paris but often visited the grandparents and my parents too in later years, because my parents and the brothers had spent their youthful years, with all their joys and sorrows, together. My father told me that the three Landsberger brothers sometimes worked as actors on the wooden stages of popular theaters outside Berlin, in Schöneberg or Pankow or some other place. At an opportune moment, one of them would jump up on the stage and declaim or sing Classical or Berlin-Comic songs, and the audience would sing along with them. All their performances were unrehearsed, lusty naturalistic performances that grew out of their own experiences and emotions.

And then 1848![61] How that had aroused the minds of young men! When the Revolution broke out, the brothers wanted to do

---

[60] Jenny herself married Philipp Bornstein (1843–1891), her father's business associate and later partner. Philipp was sixteen years older than Jenny. Such marriages were common in family-owned businesses (Jenny's sister Hanne married Israel Barth's business associate Wilhelm Bütow). Jenny, however, presents her engagement and marriage to Philipp as a genuine love match.

[61] The Revolution (or Revolutions) of 1848 were middle-class uprisings directed against the hereditary nobility that ruled the many German states.

their part too. In Berlin they helped build barricades and defended them with stones, fought in the front ranks against the Army, and assisted the wounded. The bitterest battle was at the corner of Taubenstrasse and Friedrichstrasse,[62] where the defenders of the barricade suffered their biggest losses. All three brothers were there among the citizens. There was no "German Race" then, no Jews, only Berliners with their "*ick*" and "*dett*" and "*kike mal*,"[63] young men and old men who yearned to breathe the air of freedom.

My father told me proudly, "On March 18 we brought out the coffins of the fallen and, followed by the citizenry of Berlin, marched to the royal palace. We stopped there and the crowd shouted, 'Come out!' The king[64] came out onto the balcony wearing a hat. The people bellowed, 'Take off your hat!' The king removed his hat, and the coffins were slowly paraded before him and then given a dignified burial in Friedrichshain."[65]

I myself remember that on the anniversary observance for those who fell in March 1848, the people of Berlin would go to Friedrichshain and decorate the graves. Under the Socialist

---

These uprisings were inspired by the Enlightenment, the French Revolution and Napoleon. Most of Germany was affected by them. After initial successes, the Revolution failed, but it laid the groundwork for later political reforms.

[62] This intersection is located in central Berlin, close to where Jenny's family later lived.

[63] Berlin dialect: "*ick*" and "*dett*" = "I" and "that;" "*kike mal*" means "look there."

[64] This was King Frederick William IV of Prussia (ruled 1840–1861).

[65] Friedrichshain ("Frederick's Grove") is a Berlin neighborhood. Its Volkspark was inaugurated in 1840 to mark the hundredth anniversary of Frederick the Great's becoming king of Prussia.

government after 1918, representatives of the Socialist Party delivered solemn speeches there and at the end of the ceremony patriotic songs were sung and classical music (Beethoven's Funeral March) was played.

GOVERNESSES –
AGE FOUR

W hile Governess I was in charge of the household, she did nothing for my sister; she let her do whatever she wanted. She did not help Hanne with her schoolwork and paid no attention to what my sister, now ten years old, did when she had free time. I knew quite well what Hanne was doing. She would often tell me some fantastic story straight out of *The Thousand and One Nights*. If we were walking across the parade ground near Kroll's establishment, Hanne would say that those were her soldiers who did an about-face in front of her; if an officer put his hand to his cap, Hanne would say that he was greeting her, and so on. At night after everyone else was asleep, her carriage would pick her up and take her to the king's castle. Old General "Papa" Wrangel[66] came to visit us on Behrenstrasse only to see her — and if he threw a shiny copper three-penny coin to the street urchin who ran after us, it

---

[66] General Friedrich von Wrangel (1784-1877), a career officer who commanded the Prussian army in the war with Denmark in 1864. Often called "Papa Wrangel" because of his age, he was one of Israel Barth's political-military contacts. Family lore has it that Israel Barth's textiles and clothing business boomed in the 1860s when it began furnishing cloth for Prussian army uniforms.

was Hanne who had told the General to do so. Hanne was full of these stories, and according to her, all the children with whom she played or went ice skating or for a treat at Buchohlz's Café — they were all her pages.

I believed everything she said, but I did not think long and hard about her stories. I thought they were interesting, but they didn't mean a great deal to me. When Hanne was eleven or twelve, she talked Papa into letting her have dancing lessons. Sometimes the governess accompanied her; I didn't go, but I got free dancing lessons from her when she came home.

While we had the first governess, I could also do what I pleased. Unfortunately, my morning hours with Papa fell by the wayside, and so did most of our evening games. Instead, Papa now read, went out, smoked, and didn't say very much.

Still, my mornings and afternoons were much as before. Papa and I still had our afternoon walks in the Tiergarten. Unfortunately Aunt Solomon and Aunt Bley moved away around this time, to a flat far away from us, near Friedrichstrasse. After a while we finally got permission to go visit them perhaps twice a month. Hanne and I were also able to meet Mama there. I do not have many happy memories from these visits. Suddenly everything seemed very different, and I just did not understand what had happened. Hannchen, who probably understood the situation quite well, got upset before each visit and warned me not to ask any questions, or else we would be in a lot of trouble. As a result, we both became very anxious.

During one of our visits, I happened to say that we had a new neighbor and her brother living across the hall from us and that Papa called her "Sternluise" because she was Fräulein Luise

Stern from Vienna. Luise could sing beautiful songs, for example, "The Farmer Has a Pigeon House."

"Oh, those Viennese songs," said Mama.

"She has other ones, too," I said, "like this one." Then I sang:

The earth needs rain, the sun needs light,
The sky needs stars when night falls,
The little bird needs a branch to build its nest,
A person needs a heart to which he can trust his own.
Tra la lai la.[67]

Then Mama suddenly said angrily, "Stop it, I can't stand those songs!"

On the way home Hanne bawled me out. I had no idea why I shouldn't have said anything. "You," Hanne said, "would probably have kept on running at the mouth and told her how Fräulein Stern's fancy makeup amused Papa, and that Fräulein Stern said to him: 'Well, mister, dolls do have to put on makeup, don't they?'"

"Well, Hannchen," I said, "why shouldn't I have told it? After all, didn't Papa laugh, and didn't the governess laugh too when Papa told her the story?"

Hanne replied, "You are really dumb," and pointed to her forehead with her finger.

Governess I also nearly ended our young lives, and her own, by carbon monoxide poisoning. Hanne and I slept with the governess in a room with two windows; Papa slept in a nearby alcove. One winter night I woke up and had to throw up. That

---

[67] All this in Viennese dialect.

was not unusual because I often had an upset stomach due to hereditary constipation. When I couldn't stop throwing up, Papa woke up, came into the room and immediately took me into the dining room. He threw open all the windows despite the cold outside. He woke the maid and sent her at once to get the doctor. I don't know what the doctor did with Hanne and the governess. I was sitting in a big overstuffed chair next to an open window in the dining room, and was urged to keep puking into a bowl — the more the better. For some time after this incident, Papa and the three of us took hours-long afternoon rides through the Tiergarten in an open carriage.

That was the end of Governess I. Governess II appeared on the scene shortly afterward, probably around April 1865.[68] She was younger than the first one, and like her was a Christian, but more of a teacher than her predecessor. She was not especially interested in keeping the flat clean. Papa once even wrote a message on the piano cover: "Here's dust to be wiped up." Grandmother was not pleased with the cleanliness of our clothing, underwear or ears when we visited her. But the governess did keep Hanne relatively clean, and demanded that she take piano lessons from Herr Mietzke, her "cousin." Later this governess started to teach me to read, write, count and add. I have no idea whether she taught me well or badly; I just remember that I wanted to be done with my lessons quickly and go play outside. Around this time, unfortunately, Paul Konström became crazy about reading, and I wasn't able to read with him. He would badger me and hand me his story book: "Hey kiddo,

---

[68] Jenny erroneously writes "1867."

read a little, can't you?" And I couldn't. So I was upset, but there was nothing I could do.

The rear of our building gave on to the Royal Bakery on Französischerstrasse. Now and then, when the baker boys would see us playing outside, they would throw little bags of delicious pastry over to us. That was for us little girls. Eventually Hannchen and Minchen Konström discovered our treasure trove. When the boys saw the older girls, they tossed over even more bags of fresh pastry. At one point, these pastry artists demanded kisses for their gifts. If the girls stood on top of the trash heap, the boys could kiss them over the fence. First Minchen offered her little sister, Cielchen. The baker boys rejected her and asked for the older girls instead. After some back and forth, the older girls stood on the trash pile! This went on for weeks. However, one day Grandma Beersohn, the innkeeper's wife, saw what was going on and immediately told Papa and the Konströms. They in turn went in person to the royal baker and informed him of the "offer and payment," and then and there our source of sweets was shut off. I do not know if the older girls (aged twelve to fourteen) were given a talking-to. But I can tell you that those sweets were better than any I ever ate later in life. Was that due to the fact that "stolen fruits are the sweetest?"

We gradually found out that the Governess II was not perfect either. I spent more time playing outside, and was at loose ends. I knew all the fables by heart. But could I read real books? And where would I get them? One day, as usual, I brought in the newspaper for Papa. I had never tried to read it, but I was so bored that I looked at the headlines and was able to make out

"*Volks-Zeitung*,"[69] and below that "The Newspaper for Everyone."

"Papa, I can read!" I cried. "Papa, what is a newspaper?" Papa laughed and gave me a short explanation. The next day he gave me a copy of Andersen's fairy tales.[70] Now I was able to say to Paul, "Hey kiddo, I have something you don't." So we made a deal: "If you lend me your book, I'll lend you mine." And I was never bored any longer.

In that same year the war with Denmark[71] broke out. The women in our household all sat around the big dining table tearing up big strips of linen to make piles of bandages. I naturally wanted to help, since that was what the older girls were doing. I have to admit that my pile of bandages was very small and somewhat grubby; I hope they threw it away. Berlin was filled with military units in transit, lots of soldiers and military music, with which we children joined in. The march "Schleswig-Holstein, Surrounded by the Sea" was our favorite. But since we didn't know any geography we sang, "Schleswig-Holstein stomps on the wall," and we would stamp our little feet to the tune.

It was a very short war. We children began to play war outside, using the scrap boards from Herr Schleip's business even though he didn't like it. Then the troops returned to Berlin, and we watched them from the window of Herr Venat's

---

[69] The *Berliner Volks-Zeitung* ("People's Newspaper") was founded in 1853. It was a large-circulation newspaper with an explicit liberal and democratic outlook.

[70] This book's co-editor Olga Wise remembers that Jenny gave the Bornstein great-grandchildren (herself included) a copy of Andersen's fairy tales.

[71] Prussian–Danish war of 1864. After its victory, Prussia annexed the Danish provinces of Schleswig and Holstein, which are still part of Germany today.

establishment, in which we had put chairs so we could see better. Herr Venat was the royal hairdresser and Papa's neighbor.[72]

Once a week, Governess II took me along on an afternoon visit to her aunt. I cannot tell you how much I hated this. First we had to go by foot up over Charlottenstrasse and then to Lindenstrasse; then I had to sit still upstairs and be quiet. The governess spoke to a woman, and then her "cousin" Mietzke appeared. The governess would disappear with him for a long time; it seemed like an eternity to me before she reappeared. Then she hurried back home with me. That went on for several months. Since I was now a little older and less naive, one day when Papa and I were strolling in the Tiergarten, I told him how much I hated those visits. And so I was freed from my weekly torture. Now I could either play outside with the neighbor children or go to Papa's store while the governess made her visits. Sometimes Papa would send me to visit Uncle Jonas Speyer's children. I liked that. The children had wonderful tin soldiers along with all the accompanying military gear — even ambulances and carts for carrying off the dead. We stormed the Danish fortifications with shout and song. We only quarreled when they kept saddling me with the Danish soldiers. I wanted to win at least once, so I grabbed the Prussian soldiers, the victors! In this way we passed the time together.

Now I come back to our last days with a governess in the house.[73] Our friends the Giehlers had rented a plot with an arbor

---

[72] Probably meaning that their businesses were located next to or near each other.

[73] The two vignettes narrated in this paragraph and the following one have been moved forward from their original position in the manuscript.

in Jungfern Park.[74] I could go there with my friend Hanna Giehler. We would play, plant seed potatoes in the ground, and water them. When July came, the new potatoes were ripe. Then everyone who lived at 24 Behrenstrasse (Hanne later said there were twenty-four of us) was invited to dig up the potatoes. We roasted them on the spot in charcoal braziers, and everyone dug in. How wonderful those potatoes smelled and tasted! Even today my tongue and nose remember their taste and aroma. It was a wonderful country picnic.

There was a second country picnic around this time that I will never forget, but my memory of it is nowhere as pleasant. Papa and several neighbors who lived on the corner of Friedrichstrasse and Unter den Linden went out in a country wagon to the Pichelsberg,[75] loaded down with picnic baskets. Papa took me along. I was the only child in the group because I was "such a well-behaved child." That's what people said about me, at any rate. At first everything went smoothly. I didn't skip even once, even though Hanne had predicted I would. Then lunch was served. I can still see the trees, the meadows, and the tables set before me. I was sitting quietly next to Papa, ready to dig into the food.

Suddenly Frau Heinrich let out a screech. (She was a hateful, scheming gossip who, I was later told, tried to sow discord between my parents.) "There are thirteen people at this table. One

---

[74] The Jungfernheide in Charlottenburg is a lovely park today.

[75] Pichelsberg is an area in the West End of Berlin, near the site of the Olympic Stadium from 1936. It must have been countryside during Jenny's childhood.

of us is going to die! That child has to leave!"[76] After a lot of discussion, Papa finally sat me down at a different table, so that none of the guests would have to join the ranks of the dead. There I sat all by myself, bawling my eyes out. I didn't understand in the least how I could kill someone if I sat next to Papa. Then everyone started to tease Papa about his "well-behaved" child. He told me sternly to stop crying, but I kept on howling. He didn't understand why I was so upset, nor did he explain the business of "thirteen at the table"[77] to me. Then he did something he had never done before — he slapped me. I was amazed and shocked, and stopped crying. But I became obstinate — I would not eat and I would not sing. This excursion taught me something, and I think Papa learned something too. I never saw Frau Heinrich again.

---

[76] Olga Wise remembers her great-grandmother Jenny telling her this story when she was a child.

[77] A superstition connected with the number thirteen.

DIVORCE – BELLA'S TRAGEDY

O ne day I was sitting under the trumeau mirror in the formal room and playing with a little stuffed dog (it had been Hanne's pet when it was alive) when I overheard the governess talking with Sternluise and the maid. I heard the name "Barth" spoken, so I pricked up my ears. "Yes," said one of the three, "Herr Barth absolutely would not give up the children. When it came time for the oath,[78] the man[79] stuck his feet out so that Herr Barth almost fell over." (There were sounds of general astonishment.) "But now the marriage is over."

A few days or weeks later Hannchen and I went to Aunt Solomon's house to visit Mama, as provided in the divorce decree. As we finished our visit and were going down the stairs, a tall man came up the stairs and stopped on the top step. Mama said to me, "Give the gentleman your hand and say hello. He is your new father."

"My father is at home," I said. "I don't need a new father!" That is exactly how the words burst out of my mouth. Nothing further was said. I ran down the steps and Hannchen did too.

---

[78] Oath or declaration of divorce; the manuscript does not make it clear whether we are dealing with a civil divorce or a religious (Jewish) divorce.

[79] Bella's soon-to-be second husband.

When we came to 24 Behrenstrasse, Hannchen said: "Don't tell anybody anything about this."

A few months later we visited Mama in her new apartment on Friedrichstrasse, near the Weidendamm Bridge.[80] The rooms seemed small and depressing to me. Mama had married the tall, dark man. We only saw him once ever again. That was when we were called to Mama's deathbed in Dresden at the end of February 1880.[81] Hannchen and I found a drunken man standing before our dying mother's bed. She was trying to push him away. There were four good-looking children in the room also; some of them looked just like Grandfather, especially the daughters and little Julius, who was between one and two.[82] Mama pointed to the children, especially her youngest. I nodded, understanding what she meant. We contacted Mrs. Mehrländer, the president of the Jewish welfare organization in Dresden.[83] She was a distant relative and very helpful. My fiancé, Philipp,[84] often traveled to Dresden[85] on business and, together with her, saw that the children were supported financially and received an education. I

---

[80] Friedrichstrasse crosses the Spree River, Berlin's central waterway, at the Weidendamm Bridge. The bridge was famous for its ornate ironwork.

[81] At this point Jenny is twenty years old and is engaged to Philipp Bornstein.

[82] In a footnote added to her manuscript in 1946, Jenny states, "Three of these children, now in their sixties, are said to be here in the United States, but up to now I have not been able to locate them."

[83] Many Jewish welfare organizations existed in Imperial Germany, providing services to the Jewish *Gemeinde* (communities) in cities, towns and villages.

[84] Philipp Bornstein, whom Jenny married in 1880.

[85] Dresden, capital of Saxony, was one of the richest cities in eastern Germany. It was completely destroyed by Allied bombs in WWII. Many of its architectural treasures were restored after the reunification of Germany in 1990.

had hoped that Philipp and I could bring Julius into our household after we married, but Philipp said this was impossible because of Papa's attitude.

Frau Mehrländer told us that for the last six to eight years Mama had sat for hours at her needlepoint frame so that she could earn enough money to feed her family. Her husband's work as a real estate agent did not bring in any money, and he gave himself over to drink. When Mama did have a little money, he would threaten her and make her give it to him. Mama wasn't able to get any help from her parents, even though she wrote them letters and visited them. Grandfather's second wife[86] hated Mama, and people such as Frau Heinrich and Frau Urbach, who belonged to a very strict religious congregation, told Grandfather slanderous stories about Bella's behavior until he believed everything they told him.

"Bella is exaggerating," they said. "Bella's children are better dressed than my nieces."

"Bella has money for her husband's alcohol."

"Bella even gives things to the poor; Fanny Treuherz told me, and she works in the Jewish welfare office."

Hanne and I visited our grandparents several times over the next half-dozen years to ask them to help, because Mama's letters from Dresden made it clear that she was in great need. However, there we hit a stone wall. Grandfather's second wife knew how to set her husband against his daughter. She would say things like: "She doesn't keep a kosher household, she's always spent money

---

[86] This is the same grandmother who is presented in a more sympathetic light earlier in the memoir.

carelessly, and just ask her if she goes to synagogue or fasts on Yom Kippur." (I can tell you that she surely did fast, and more than once a year, too, since she often had to go without food so her children could eat!)

Hanne and I saved every penny we could for Mama. Hanne darned Uncle David's socks at five pfennigs a pair. My own allowance was fifty pfennigs a month. To save money I drank coffee without sugar (sugar was expensive then). We sent her our birthday and Christmas money. But all this added up to only eighty or ninety marks a year we could send to Dresden — even if we included part of Hanne's monthly allowance of three marks. When Father came back from Karlsbad[87] and gave us money, we used it to buy birthday presents for our parents and for Paula. Uncle Siegmund (my stepmother Therese's brother) also helped out with money sometimes while he was still unmarried and living with us. Uncle Siegmund was a lovely and generous man, and the uncle I loved best. I owe him a great deal for what he taught me about sensibility and literature.

Frau Mehrländer had written us that in November Mama had come down with severe influenza and inflammation of the lungs. Despite her doctor's warning, she had left her sick bed all too soon to work because "she had to have money." Frau Mehrländer wrote that Mama had gone out on foot in the cold winter weather to deliver her handiwork to stores in person, and that she had now

---

[87] Karlsbad, located about 100 kilometers outside Prague, is a well-known spa (*Bad*), famous for its thermal waters. In the nineteenth century it was the foremost spa in Europe. Part of the lifestyle of the well-to-do middle class involved "taking the cure" or "taking the waters" annually at a spa like Karlsbad.

been in bed for two or three weeks with galloping consumption. The doctor had given up all hope. When we went to her, we took along fresh food and remedies that we hoped would restore her strength. Unfortunately I couldn't get Father's permission to stay in Dresden with Mama to the end; he was afraid I might also get infected. Frau Mehrländer promised to look in on Mama and to write us with any news. Two days later Mama was dead.

What a horribly wasted life! It might have turned out very differently if Mama's own mother, Johanna, had not died during Mama's stormy adolescent years. Perhaps she could have shaped Mama's unbridled temperament and seen to it that her character developed in a healthy way. Once when I was with Mama, I looked at her fine-featured face and read in her expression that she was painfully aware that she had carelessly ruined her life. This was when she was visiting in Berlin, and against our better judgment, we took her to see our house on Grossbeerenstrasse. The building had twenty-three windows and a huge garden. She asked, "Which floor do you live on?"

"On the first floor,"[88] replied Hanne in a soft voice. We saw how Mama's expression changed. Her face suddenly looked distressed and frozen. Was she condemning herself? I looked up at our house in surprise. The gas lights were burning in the three front rooms and the window shades were up, so it was possible to get a view of the interior rooms. I realized that it took everything she had to tell us, "Adieu. I'll see you tomorrow. Get home safely."

---

[88] In European terminology, the "first" floor is the floor above the street or ground floor; in American terms, it is the "second" floor.

"If she had only waited for a couple of years after the divorce," Papa said to our stepmother when he heard of Mama's death. "I missed her so much. We could have started a new life together." I think our stepmother, Therese, who was both perceptive and tactful, told us what Papa said so that we could free our hearts and minds from our sad thoughts about Mama. And in this she was successful.

PAPA REMARRIES

One morning shortly before my sixth birthday, Papa sent Carl to the house. "Papa wants Jenny to get dressed and come to the store." In the morning? This was very unusual. So I went.

Papa called for a droschke and said that we were going to visit the Rosins. (Dr. Rosin was Father's cousin and a rabbi.) I would have preferred to walk in the Tiergarten with Papa; Frau Rosin always found fault with the way I played with their son Heinz (as an adult he became Professor Rosin), who was two years younger than I.

When we arrived, Dr. Rosin was very nice to me, as always. Frau Rosin let Heinz and me go into a nearby room and play. After a bit, a tall lady wearing a white apron came into the room along with a maidservant. The two were carrying a gigantic basket of clean laundry, which they sorted and placed in a nearby chest. Heinrich and I ran around the basket; he tried to catch my hair, we rolled around and laughed and played hide-and-seek between the table and chairs shouting, "Hallo," and, "Come find me." The tall lady looked at us, now and then, but didn't say anything.

Finally Dr. Rosin and Papa came into the room, and said that we were going to leave now.

"Did you say good day to Auntie?"[89] they asked.

"She wasn't in the room when we came in."

Much laughter on the part of the three adults. "Well, now you must say adieu to Auntie."

And so I did with a bow and a curtsy as Heinz tried to pull my hair one last time. This was the first time I met Aunt Therese,[90] who would become my second mother.

From then on, during the winter of 1865, there was a lot of whispering between Governess II, Sternluise and the servant girls. I didn't pay much attention and Hanne didn't seem to notice anything different. Our Mama had moved to Dresden and at Christmas we received a large package from her. Hannchen got ribbons; I got doll dishes, all very elegant. Hannchen and I went ice skating. Hanne always had a bunch of boys hanging around her, and she was a strong skater, whereas I was a very tentative skater and couldn't keep up. I quickly got cold and went home.

It was early February 1866 when Papa told the governess that Fräulein Simon-Meyer was going to be dining with us, and to put everything in order. I was not in the least interested. I was scrubbed up, my hair was combed, and my dress was changed, all of which I found annoying. Hanne, who was about to turn thirteen, was especially mean to me. Finally it was dinnertime. I have no idea what we ate. Everyone was very quiet and inhibited; I dared not say a word. I had immediately recognized the woman we saw at Rosin's house earlier, and curtsied and said hello to

---

[89]A common way for a child to refer to a grown lady; the term does not necessarily imply kinship.

[90] Jenny's second mother was Therese Barth, née Simon-Meyer (1837–1881). She married Israel Barth in 1866.

her. Papa told us, "This is Aunt Therese." Hanne put on her sourest face; the governess was cold as ice. I had no clue what was going on.

After dinner we went into the parlor. Hanne was supposed to play the piano, but she said she was tired and wanted to go to bed. Papa and Aunt Therese sat together on the sofa. I sat across from them, but I didn't like it there because my Papa was sitting with a strange woman. Before anyone could stop me, I dived under the table, crawled over to the sofa, and climbed up between the two of them. Everyone laughed out loud. Aunt Therese stroked my head and said, "You did that very well!" Then I found my voice and began to ask questions and tell stories. Everything became quite lively. Papa said to me, "Sing something for us."

"What should I sing?"

"Sing something about springtime."

So I sang, "Springtime, springtime echoes through the forest. Let us sing and dance and jump. Spring will soon be here."[91] And indeed, Aunt Therese soon brought spring into our dreary house.

On February 15, 1866, we were invited to the Franks' house to celebrate the birthday of their daughter Fanny Rothstein. The Franks were Aunt Therese's uncle and aunt, but we didn't know that. We were quite surprised when Herr Venat came to fix our hair — even curling it with his curling iron! What was all this fuss about? When we arrived at the Franks' house with Papa, we saw an older man sitting on the sofa. He had a smile on his face. A grey-haired woman sat next to him. They were Herr and Frau

---

[91] This may be "*Frühlingslied*" ("Springtime Song") by Felix Mendelssohn (1809–1847).

Frank. Hanne and I curtsied and said hello, just as Papa wished. Then the friendly lady ran her hand over my hair and said, "You both look just lovely." The words burst out of my mouth: "Yes, just like oxen at Pentecost."[92] I can still hear the guffaws and laughter of everyone in the room. One of the men came over to me — he was tall, dark, and elegantly dressed — and lifted me over his head and asked, "Shall I set you down on top of the stove?"[93]

"Can you really do that?" I asked.

But the old man on the sofa called out: "Siegmund, really — that stove is hot."[94]

So the man put me back down.

Then Uncle Siegmund and I played hide-and-seek through the whole flat. He taught me a special dance from Vienna — the plover dance.[95]

"You'll only see that in Vienna," he said. And he sang a song to go along with the dance; I still remember the melody but not the words.

Uncle Siegmund had come from Vienna for his sister Therese's engagement. He worked in Vienna, then later in Berlin with Uncle David. Both uncles lived for some time with my parents in Berlin. It was very pleasant to have them around. We all got along beautifully. Uncle Emmanuel, who was Papa's

---

[92] Pentecost is a Christian holiday celebrated fifty days after Easter Sunday. The custom of decorating oxen with garlands at Pentecost probably derives from earlier folk festivals celebrating spring.

[93] During Jenny's childhood rooms were heated by large stoves (*Ofen*) that were often covered in decorative ceramic tiles.

[94] Uncle Siegmund is one of Therese's brothers.

[95] A plover is a bird.

brother and business assistant, lived with us too. He was the translator (English and French) for the business's foreign customers.

The next four to six weeks sped by. Governess II left in early April 1866, although she came back twice a week to take Hannchen to her piano lessons with her "cousin." Aunt Therese came to the house often. With her help, and that of Carl and the housemaids, the house was cleaned from top to bottom. Everything was washed, cleaned, and aired out; junk was tossed out or burned, and new things were brought in. Sternluise and her brother hauled away old furniture, and new furniture appeared in almost every room, even the kitchen. Hannchen and I got our old bedrooms back. Aunt Therese worked energetically, overseeing the project and setting the example for her helpers. At one point I got nauseous as we were cleaning the toilet in the bathroom. I shouted: "Auntie, this crud is older than time. Forget about it!" Later people would sometimes tease me by saying, "Tell me, Jenny, is that crud older than time?"

As we worked together, Aunt Therese told me how I was going to be helping her with household work. I told her how much I dreaded it when the governess and the maid would leave to go shopping, leaving me alone in the apartment on days the weather was bad (if the weather was good I was outside playing with the neighborhood children). They locked the front and back doors and took the keys with them, but still. . . . Then Aunt Therese said: "You'll never have to worry about that again. When I go grocery shopping, you will come along with me. I'm going to give you your very own little basket with a mesh bag inside. You'll learn how to pick out good food for the household. I promise you."

A few days before April 15, Frau Urbach came to visit. Hannchen and I exchanged glances. Hannchen usually disappeared so she wouldn't have to be around her. I just stared. I have never met anyone as abrasive, strict and self-important as she was. That day she was really dressed up. I watched her preening herself in front of the mirror. She stuck a big purple ostrich feather in her dark hair.

I said, "Auntie Urbach, you look all fancy today; where are you going?"

She answered, "Don't you know that your father is getting married today?"

My response: "No, I didn't know that; can't you take me along?"

She: "Don't be silly — you don't belong there."

"Why not, Auntie?"

"Because you have no sense of manners whatsoever," she said.

I don't recall how I spent the afternoon. In the evening, when the servant girl said it was time for me to go to bed, I said: "No!" Hanne went to bed silently. I hated it all. But suddenly the servant girl lit the large oil lamp, put on a fresh white apron, and looked out the window. I looked out too. A carriage stopped in front of the house. The servant girl and I, with the oil lamp, hurried down the three flights of stairs, as Papa and Aunt Therese walked in through the front door. Papa seemed neither surprised nor upset to see me. He said to me in a friendly voice: "Aunt Therese is going to be the mother in this house now." I saw how

Aunt Therese's long white train swept across the floor.[96] I gathered the ends of her train in both hands as, leaning on Father's arm, she walked with him up to our flat. I walked behind them, like a page, holding the train high off the ground. "Good night, comrade," Papa sang to me softly, to the tune of the well-known song. I went to bed, my heart filled with happiness.

The day after the wedding we had the Lendemain party.[97] I had never heard of that kind of party before. We children had often watched the wedding processions of bridal couples and their guests, and even the marriage ceremony itself, at the nearby Dreifaltigkeitskirche.[98] When we were outside playing on Behrenstrasse, we would see people dressed in wedding clothes, and we would dash through Kanonierstrasse and be over at the church and the wedding carriage in an instant. But a Lendemain — what was that?

In the afternoon my new mama and Venat the royal hairdresser made an appearance, both of them wearing hairdresser's robes. I watched in amazement. Venat fluffed and brushed Mama's hair and performed all kinds of miracles with it. When he was done, her hair cascaded in gleaming Genoese-styled locks down past the nape of her neck. Pale blue ribbons, threaded amidst her hair, formed a lofty diadem above her forehead. A décolleté white mull dress and a medallion on a golden chain completed her outfit. Her elegant figure made a

---

[96] From this point on, Jenny refers to Therese as "Mama."

[97] The French word "*lendemain*" means, literally, "the day after."

[98] Church of the Trinity.

powerful impression on me.[99] She was no fairy-tale princess — she was a real one!

A hired caterer in a tuxedo had transformed our front room into a banquet chamber for many guests. The table was decorated with flowers and candles. Food was brought out in big baskets. Papa was wearing a tuxedo too, with a white waistcoat. Then there were the four uncles, Siegmund, Emmanuel, Louis and David, plus the Rosins and many heretofore unknown uncles and aunts, Rothsteins and Urbachs. Hanne and I went off into an adjoining room. Nobody was keeping an eye on us, or even paying attention. After a speech by Rabbi Rosin (which of course I didn't understand), dinner was served. Hanne disappeared, apparently uninterested in the goings-on. After dinner, the guests sang little songs they had made up. I recall a verse or two from Uncle Siegmund's ditty:

"He fell for her at Rosins'; anything that takes a long time will be good." (I understood that.)

"Barth is looking very imperial today, because Love has crowned him."

"Emmanuel means 'God with us.' That tells us he's a great businessman, since his motto is engraved on every thaler."[100]

The guests raised their champagne glasses to this, and later Uncle Siegmund toasted the ladies in verse. Then I must have fallen asleep, because I don't remember anything more.

---

[99] Portions of this sentence are indecipherable in Jenny's manuscript.

[100] The *Vereinsthaler* (or simply "thaler") was the unit of currency in pre-Imperial Germany. The border of this coin was engraved with the Prussian motto *Gott mit uns* ("God with us").

~~ ~~

MY SECOND MAMA –
THERESE

I started to take an interest in the household now that my new Mama was in charge. I saw how clean and lovely she kept everything. I tried to help her, so I spent less time playing with my friends, feeding the horses, and so on. My afternoon walks with Papa continued, but now Mama came along. Papa sang and declaimed as before. However, my morning visits with him came to an end. I suppose I had gotten too old for my honey cake and special conversations. When the weather was bad, Mama had me read aloud and practice my multiplication tables, from 1 x 1 to 6 x 6.

One day Frau Schlesinger came to visit. She was a rich elderly spinster whom Mama had served for years as a companion. She visited often and was greeted ceremoniously. Mama usually knitted during Frau Schlesinger's visits and listened to her prattle on. Mostly they talked about housekeeping and raising children. I found her sermons disgusting. Hanne disappeared as soon as she arrived. One day Frau Schlesinger suddenly said: "The child is over six years old and runs around without doing anything. Why isn't she knitting? If she doesn't know how, it's your job to teach her."

And so it was. Rain or shine, I had to knit with four needles, working by the sweat of my brow. It was very, very hard. One day I got really angry. It was afternoon, and the sunshine was smiling at me. I was so upset and fed up with knitting that I kept dropping stitches. Mama said consolingly, "Come here child. I'll show you how to fix this." She did this three or four times. I suddenly lost all patience. Before Mama could stop me, I threw my knitting to the floor and ran out the door shouting, "I'll show you how I go take a walk!" And then I was out the door.

I wound up at Papa's store; he saw how angry I was and understood that I needed to be outside in the fresh air. (When Papa was still healthy, he was a person who absolutely had to walk for hours and hours, so he knew exactly what I needed at that moment.) He asked Carl to bring him his hat and cane. There was not one word of reproach. We walked our usual route in the Tiergarten at a comfortable pace, enjoying the fresh green of early spring. We shook the ladybugs off of the fresh shoots of the birch trees, singing "Chimneysweep and Kaiser."[101] When we got behind the tents,[102] I began to sing: "Ladybug, fly away. Your father's off at war. Your mother is in Pomerania,[103] Pomerania has all burned down. Ladybug, fly away." Almost all my ladybugs flew off. Then Papa and I went down to the water. He plucked the blades of grass that were best for blowing and whistling, and we walked to the lake playing on our new musical instruments. It was an indescribably marvelous time. How our

---

[101] A "chimneysweep" is a ladybug that is dark all over; a "kaiser" has a red head and a reddish abdomen.

[102] As already noted, a section of the Tiergarten contained large tents, available for rental by the public. Middle-class Berliners often preferred these tents to their stifling flats and houses during the summer.

[103] A province in northeastern Prussia, on the Baltic.

outing was reported at home, *"non so."*[104] All I know is that I no longer had to knit at home. (Later when I was in school, two or three of the crafts teachers, who had not yet taken their exams, took my knitting paraphernalia away and instead gave me a story book so I could read aloud to them while they worked. This was a customary practice in workshops at that time. I was delighted with my punishment.)

A few weeks later Uncle Siegmund came to visit from Vienna. For some reason he and Mama decided to visit Sandersleben,[105] where they had been born, and I was allowed to come along. This was my first trip ever. We were going to spend two or three days in Sandersleben so Mama packed four dresses for me. I was surprised at this.[106] When I told Mama, she just laughed — I think she had an idea what kind of trouble her little girl could get into in a new place.

The train trip to Nordhausen[107] went smoothly. Then came the ride in the mail coach. I was astounded by all the beautiful gold flowers — the fields looked like a golden dress. We rode along tree-lined streets and roads. It became quite warm. I took off my knitted yellow gloves, and one of them fell out of the window.

"Driver, driver," Mama called out. "Stop!"

---

[104] Italian: "I don't know."

[105] Sandersleben is a small town southwest from Berlin in Saxony-Anhalt, east of the Harz Mountains.

[106] A lot of dresses for a short trip, keeping in mind that people did not change clothes daily.

[107] Nordhausen is a town in the eastern Harz Mountains, not far from Sandersleben.

The coach stopped, and Uncle Siegmund jumped out and retrieved my glove. After a while I let the other glove drop out the window.

"Driver, driver," Mama called again. "Stop."

The carriage stopped, and Uncle Siegmund again jumped out and rescued my glove. This was a really amusing game! But the third time I threw a glove out the window, Mama said, "Enough! If you do that once more I will have to punish you. And you know I keep my word."

My response was: "You keep your word? Didn't you promise me months ago that you would give me a little basket with a net bag inside it?"

Mama thought for a bit and said, "You are right, my child, I forgot all about my promise. As soon as we get to Sandersleben we'll buy one." And so we did. That was a good lesson; it taught me that it is important to keep your promises, even when it is to your own disadvantage.

In Sandersleben, a tiny farming village, everyone was delighted to see us. We were welcomed all around by Aunt Frank (née Meyer), her husband, and their grown sons and daughters. They soon went to the "good place"[108] with Mama, Uncle Siegmund, and Mama's sister Aunt Anna, who had come up from Sondershausen[109] with her son Leopold. Leopold was two years younger than I. While the grown-ups were away, we wandered around outside. We came upon a meadow with a small brook

---

[108] Presumably the cemetery.

[109] Sondershausen is a town in the state of Hesse, near Kassel. Jenny writes both "Sondershausen" and "Sandershausen" (the latter is a village now inside Kassel's city limits). The editors belive Sondershausen is correct.

running through it. Small clean stones peeked above the water. I sprang from rock to rock. Leopold shouted: "Look out — you'll fall!" I turned around to look at him (he was still on the footpath) and plop — I landed in the brook. When Mama saw me later, she just smiled and let me go to bed with a snack.

The next day I wore my second dress. It was the Sabbath, celebrated the way it was at my grandparents' house. After lunch there was apple cake for dessert. I started to eat a slice, but stopped immediately.

"Now," said my aunt, "eat your slice of cake."

"Oh Auntie," I said, "this cake tastes like oil. Mama's cake doesn't."

Mama looked at me sternly and said: "This apple cake is made the way the pious Jews still make it in the Promised Land. The olive trees that grow there produce the finest oil, which is even healthier than goose grease.[110] Now be good and eat your cake." I got Mama's point and choked down the rest of the cake. Later, when I was out of sight, I threw it all up — and that was the end of my second clean dress.

The next day Uncle Frank gave me all kinds of ribbons from his store for me and my dolls. We all walked up to a little hill outside town. The path was lined with cherry trees, loaded with fresh ripe fruit. I had never seen anything like it. Leopold and I ran ahead. There was one tree that was lower than the others, and I tried to climb it. A man coming up the path saw me and helped me up, telling me that he was making me a gift of the tree and

---

[110] European Jews typically used goose fat instead of lard (not kosher) or butter for cooking.

that I could take all the cherries I wanted. And that is exactly what I did. By the time Mama and with the others caught up with us, my dress and I were smeared with cherries. I had also thrown some fruit down to Leopold, but he was more careful than I. Well, at least I had dress number four to wear on the trip home the next day. Then I sat with the grownups and sang songs, and later Leopold and I played some more. I have lovely memories of my first trip and of the old people in Sandersleben.

July 1866. War.[111] Making bandages again. Eating raw fruit was absolutely forbidden. Cholera! Drinking water had to be boiled (and we didn't have an icebox). When we were around Mama we followed these instructions to the letter, but when we went over to the Konströms we were offered heaps of forbidden fruit every day. I loved fruit, but I restrained myself while the Konström children ate merrily away. I didn't get sick, and neither did they. Many people did die, however, especially among the troops deployed at Königgratz.[112] (My husband Philipp also fell sick after a night watch in the forest outside Königgratz, but survived.)

---

[111] This is the war of 1866 between Prussia and Austria for leadership of the German Confederation.

[112] Königgratz, in Bohemia, was the site of the decisive battle of the Prussian–Austrian war of 1866.

~~~ ~~~

THE LENZ SCHOOL
FOR GIRLS

In July 1866 I turned seven. My parents decided that I had enjoyed enough freedom, and now it was time to put me in a straightjacket. Mama had a friend who taught Kranzler's children (the family owned Kranzler's pastry shop). She strongly recommended the Lenz School,[113] located on the Hausvogteiplatz, even though it was farther from our house than Hanne's school, which was right on Behrenstrasse. Mama and I went to meet the school director, Herr Lenz. I think he was about sixty years old. It was his job to decide in which of his nine classes he should place me.[114] After looking me over carefully, he asked Mama if I had learned anything yet.

"Oh yes, she can read, write, do a little arithmetic, sing, and recite poetry."

---

[113] The Lenz School was a private school for well-to-do young women. Here they were taught the basics to enable them to be competent wives capable of running a large household. They also studied literature, history and languages. Jenny is unusual in that she also (after the Lenz School) obtained a certification that would enable her to become a teacher.

[114] In the German educational system in the second half of the nineteenth century, children first attended a *Volksschule* (elementary school) for four years, then a *Höhere Schule* (secondary school, of which there were different kinds) for six years. The normal graduation age was sixteen.

Herr Lenz picked up a book I had never seen before, opened it, and asked me to read aloud. I no longer remember what book it was. It seemed to me that I had to read endlessly, page after page. Then he took the book out of my hand and said, "She reads with comprehension." Then he then gave me a piece of lined paper and dictated a passage for me to write.

"That needs a lot of improvement," he said. "How are her number skills?"

I burst out, "I can add to a thousand, and I know my multiplication tables up to six times six."

Herr Lenz laughed and said to Mama, "Before school starts, do you think she can learn the multiplication tables up to twelve times twelve?"

"Certainly," said Mama.

"Well, in that case we will try her out in the seventh class, and in a half year she can go into the sixth."[115]

I wasn't interested in being moved ahead, but Mama looked pleased and bought me some apple cake at Café Buchholz on the way home. What Herr Lenz had failed to mention, however, was that the seventh class had already studied French for half a year. If he had, I might have been able to learn a little before I started school.

I won't spend much time on school. Suffice it to say that I had a hard time getting used to school discipline. We had to sit still even at breakfast time (the teachers were watching us even then), we could never chat, we had to keep our hands folded, we couldn't forget our books or homework, and last of all we had to

---

[115] The first class was the highest class.

write neatly. All that, plus we had to pay attention to everything the teacher said and asked. Why in the world did we have to do all these things?

Each week the teacher put a grade in our class book, and Mama had to sign it. She was happy with me despite my less than commendable grades, and was delighted that I got a role in the Christmas play, to which all the parents were invited. I had to recite about half a page of the Christmas story: Caesar Augustus ordered that a census of the whole world be made; Mary and Joseph went up from Nazareth, and so forth. Three other children sang Christmas songs to end the performance, and everyone prayed. Afterwards Mama said to me, "You behaved just the way you do at home. You were one of the most impudent children there!"

The following day I brought home my first grades. I had never been so happy about anything. On the way home, I took my grade book out of my book bag and waved it like a flag. When I got to the front steps, I shouted so loud and jubilantly that the other residents of the house opened their doors all the way up to the third floor.

"I've got my grades!" I ran to Mama, waving my grades in the air, and read them out loud to everyone present:

Deportment: Impudent, very restless.
Attention: Unfocused, often distracted.
Effort: Satisfactory, but homework needs to show more care.
Attendance: Late 110 times!
Religion, German, Reading, and Arithmetic: Satisfactory.
French: Unsatisfactory.
Warning: If Jenny does not make satisfactory progress in the coming months, we cannot promote her to the next class.

Mama was in shock, but I was delighted; "Look, Mama; none of my classmates has as much written in their grade book as I do. The sentences are so nice and long!" Papa didn't say a thing. But from the twentieth of December until the second of January Aunt Gertrude came to our house every day for two hours and drilled me in writing, grammar, and basic French. She also explained to me why school exists and why school rules have to be followed.

Mama's big question was this: "Jenny, you always leave home exactly a half an hour before school starts. How can it be that you always get there late? It only takes twenty minutes to walk to school!" Then the following dialogue took place.

"Mama, it was so cold that the gutters were frozen!"

"But you walk on the footpath, don't you?"

"But Mama, if they're frozen I slip and slide all the way from the Gendarmenmarkt[116] and Mohrenstrasse to Taubenstrasse."

"And then, Jenny?"

"Then I come to Bullenwinkel Corner."

"And then, Jenny?"

"Well, then I see a poor woman sitting in a doorway with a child wrapped up in a blanket."

"And what does the woman do?

"She pleads with me that she's very poor, and that the child doesn't have enough to eat."

"So do you go on to school then?"

---

[116] The Gendarmenmarkt is a large square in central Berlin. It dates from the eighteenth century, and is the site of the Konzerthaus and the French and German cathedrals.

"No, then I take my book bag off my back, give the lady something, and run to the Hausvogteiplatz."

"Do you have money to give her?"

"No, I give her my breakfast for her child."

"I see. Well, you can do that if you want, but you are never ever going to be late to school again!"

And so it was; I was never late again. When Mama laid down the law like that, there was no arguing with her. Fortunately, school got easier with spring and summer, and Aunt Gertrude's tutoring began to bear fruit. I will give you an example. When the teacher handed back the first homework I turned in after Aunt Gertrude began tutoring me, she said sharply, "Barth, come here."

I walked up to her desk apprehensively.

"Who did your homework?"

"I did."

"Go to your desk and come back up to the first row with your notebook. Copy these two rows from your textbook into your notebook." I copied, and handed the notebook to her.

Then she said, "If you can write like this, why have you been giving me such sloppy work all these months?"

"Well," I said, "Aunt Gertrude just showed me over vacation how to do it correctly."

FAMILY LIFE

A fter the start of school in 1867, I had to go to Papa's store every day after lunch and do my homework in the blue back room. Papa paid close attention to my work. When I was done, we went to the Tiergarten. We usually went to the Moabit Meadow now, because that was where the stork was going to bring me the little brother I had been wanting for months.

Mama is sitting at dusk on the sofa knitting a little red dress for me; I am sitting close beside her. I notice she has become much rounder than before; I pat her "broad line" and say to her happily, "Mama, you've gotten a lot bigger. Do you like that?" She smiles at me, puts down her knitting and gives me a hug. I gather my courage and ask another question: "Mama, you are so young and Papa is so old; why did you marry such an old man?"

"Because I felt sorry for you and your sister," she said in a soft and serious voice. Those were her exact words. I didn't understand the deeper meaning of the words, but I felt a deep gratitude; her answer moved me so intensely that I asked no more questions and just sat quietly beside her.

Papa always seemed old to me even though he did not have a single white hair. It was probably because he had a slow and heavy gait. In reality, he was between forty-one and forty-three at this time, Mama around thirty. Mama said that she was twenty-seven, but later Aunt Anna told me that she, not Therese, was the youngest.[117]

A little sister was born on January 4, 1867.[118] The stork also brought Hanne and me a bag of sweets. I played with my candy while I sat at the window in the room where Mama lay in bed. I remember that I made rows and towers with my candies, but I was distracted. Poor, sick Mama; the doctor had had to perform surgery on her.[119] I had so many new things to get used to: the new nursemaid, bathing the child, feeding it, changing its diapers, and so on — and all these things were puzzling to me. When I was older, Mama told me what had happened with the sweets. As soon as Hanne came home from school (she had to return to school on January 3, I on January 9) she walked over to me at the window and asked, "Jenny, shouldn't we share the candy?"

"Yes, go ahead and divide it up," I said, paying no attention. Mama said that this scene repeated itself over and over in the next few days until there was no more candy left to divide.

I also played at the windowsill with silk paper, dolls and pencils. First I cut a doll from heavy paper. I would paint a face with a nose, etc., and then make clothing for it out of the silk paper Uncle Louis gave me. The dresses were completely à la mode. I had an entire doll family, with bag and baggage. Pencils

---

[117] Therese, born in 1837, was twenty-eight or twenty-nine when she married Israel. She had good reason to minimize her age. In Jenny's Germany, an unmarried woman who had reached the age of twenty-five was likely to be an old maid (usually because her family was too poor to give her a decent dowry), unless she married a widower.

[118] Paula Barth (1867–1942).

[119] Jenny writes, literally, that the doctor "had cut open her breast," (probably to treat an abscess).

became Papa and uncles; smaller sticks became children. I made the members of my doll family speak and act the way I had seen people do, and sometimes the way that characters in fairy stories spoke and acted. I made up fantastic stories as I walked to school, walking along close next to the houses so I wouldn't have to step out of the way of the people coming toward me. Sometimes I also made up stories as I was falling asleep. I didn't tell them to anyone, because I knew they were silly.

On December 10, 1869, a little brother was born. Everyone was overjoyed, and the birth was celebrated with all rituals[120] and ceremony. We hired a good stout nursemaid at once, but the child did not thrive the way Paula had. I was very interested in the baby and the nursemaid. Since I believed my little brother was thinking and learning as he drank in her milk, I brought her the book I had asked for and received for Christmas, Grube's *Pictures from History*.[121] But when I showed her the pictures from Greek history and began to read aloud about Troy, she said to me: "Jennyken, why on earth would I care about those old Greeks?"[122] I was astounded. There really were people who knew nothing and didn't want to know anything about the ancient Greeks! I was equally amazed by my parents' cheerful laughter when I told them at dinner, indignantly, what the nursemaid had said to me.

At the beginning of 1870 my sister Hanne became very ill with rheumatic fever. Her condition was so serious that for some

---

[120] When Jenny uses the word "ritual," she usually means a traditional Jewish religious ceremony or custom (here presumably circumcision).

[121] August Wilhelm Grube (1816–1884), pedagogue and writer.

[122] The nursemaid's dialect is irreproducible.

days it was not clear she would live. I have already told the story of Grandfather Landsberger's response to her illness. During this critical period, Mama took on the main nursing duties and stayed with Hanne day and night. She tried to figure out ways to get her to eat and to relieve her pain, the first by preparing special foods, the second by reconfiguring her bed to make her more comfortable. We even took the metal hoops off barrels and arranged the bedcovers over them, because Hanne's discomfort was so great that even the touch of a blanket hurt.

My sister's illness brought about a complete change in her attitude and behavior toward her stepmother. She came to regard Mama as the quintessence of love and wisdom, and treated her with respect. Father was nothing by comparison. Later when Hanne asked her to go to Papa to ask a special favor for her, Mama would smilingly refer to "those earlier days."

"Do you remember how you used to stick out your tongue, make fists and stamp your feet at me? I never took that amiss because, as a mother, I knew your bad behavior was just a sign of love. And now you've even made me into your mediator!"

As Hanne recovered from her illness, the doctor recommended fresh air for her and for our new little brother. So the family rented a summer place in Tent III (I think it was tent III, which was divided into private living spaces). This was really something. The family moved out of the flat on Behrenstrasse; Papa had purchased a house at 104 Leipzigerstrasse.[123] While we lived in the tents, Hanne got better and better. She spent all day

---

[123] This address is also in the heart of Berlin, only a few blocks from the flat on Behrenstrasse.

outside in the garden. We planted flowers and vegetables there. The garden had lots of apple trees from which we got a rich harvest. In May, however, there came a sad event; our little brother fell ill with brain fever and died. It was as if an unlucky star hung over our family — the boys always died. After our little brother's death, our parents spent a lot of time in the garden and sitting on the balcony[124] in the evening; they often took walks together in the dark.

The only one who maintained a cheerful mood was Uncle David.[125] He moved in with us and shared Uncle Emmanuel's[126] room. I can see him now, sitting on the balcony on Sunday morning, happily smoking his cigar and singing, "I am the Soha; I am the Pasha on the Behrenstrasse." (That was a hit song in those days.) Uncle David liked to drop little bags filled with wool[127] or something similar off the balcony to the street below. What fun it was to watch the passers-by pick them up, look inside and, completely disappointed with what they found, fling them back down on the pavement! Uncle David would tease Hanne and promise her five pfennigs to darn his socks or to jump as high as she could, laughing and joking all the while. I did not enjoy these little scenes. I am not sure that Hanne liked them either, but for her five pfennigs were five pfennigs. Fortunately, Uncle David did not try to play that game with me.

---

[124] Perhaps something more like a deck.

[125] Therese's brother David. Married Clara Cohn.

[126] Emmanuel (1839–1890?) was Israel's brother.

[127] Uncle David was a woolens merchant.

℥℥

1870
THE EXHILARATION
OF VICTORY

The War of 1870[128] suddenly burst in on our quiet and seclusion. This was a powerful event, even for the children. I was now in the fourth class in the Lenz School. In some subjects I was best in the class, but in others such as arithmetic, I was only mediocre or even unsatisfactory. When we were living in the tents, I had to leave for school at 7:10 a.m. in order to arrive on time. My teacher Herr August, who taught geography and history, wanted to make things easier on me. He introduced me to Grete Heidepriem, who was a student in the first class, and arranged for me to ride to school with her in her parents' sulky.[129] The Heidepriems had a villa near Tent Number IV. I only rode to school with her once — I missed walking through the Tiergarten, listening to the birds, marching through the Brandenburg Gate, watching the soldiers and reading the latest war news posted on the kiosks.[130] I was

---

[128] The Franco–Prussian War began July 19, 1870; the peace treaty ending it was signed May 10, 1871.

[129] A sulky is a one-horse carriage.

[130] These large cylindrical pillars or columns, on which news, advertising, and other printed matter were posted, were called "*Litfasssäule*," after their inventor Ernst Litfass (1816–1874).

willing to get up at six in the morning for that anytime. To have to sit in the carriage? To say thank you? Not to run and jump? Not to read the latest news? Not to enjoy the latest victory together with the people reading beside me? Oh, Fräulein Heidepriem, I feel so sorry for you!

So I would arrive at school full of the latest news. Although I liked school and paid attention because I had interesting subjects, I was impatient for classes to be over so I could run and find out the latest news. I would run like the wind to Papa's store and listen to what the smart men had to say. Then Carl, carrying Uncle Emmanuel's lunch kit (Uncle Emmanuel always ate in the store), would walk me back to the tents. On Unter den Linden there was barely room to walk. The streets were full of people every day. Carl, who was very tall, would carry me on his shoulders (my legs hung down to his chest), but no one paid attention to us or made comments about our appearance. We stopped at the kiosks and joined the crowd of people reading the latest dispatches from the front. When we came to the Pariser Platz, I bought the latest newspaper from a young paper boy. When we got to the Tiergarten, we rushed to the tents. Old Major B. would be waiting for us impatiently at the entrance to the garden. I immediately gave him the special edition of the newspaper, and after he had finished it, I took it to Mama. Sometimes in the afternoon Hanne and I went back to the Brandenburg Gate to see if there was any new information. In the evening Papa came home with various newspapers and war reports. He and the old major competed in predicting when the war would end and in speculating what the aftermath would be. This was all very exciting and wonderful to me. Everyone was sure that a victorious peace was not long away.

One September day we were in the middle of arithmetic class when Director Lenz walked into our classroom. Sedan had fallen and Napoleon III had been taken prisoner.[131] All discipline suddenly went out the window. I and the other students grabbed our book bags from our lockers, ignoring Herr Lenz's pleas for order. We put on our hats, jumped up on our desks and then back down, and ran out to Unter den Linden. Papa gave me permission to go with Carl down to the statue of Old Fritz[132] across from the palace. There were flags hanging from houses, schools, and stores everywhere we looked. All Berlin was out in the streets. The flower stores and vendors had sold out all their stock, and the statue and the entire monument was covered in flowers. A chimneysweep's boy had climbed to the top of the statue of the great man from Sans Souci[133] and hung a garland on it. Then the crowd began to sing patriotic songs: "Hail to Thee in Victor's Crown"[134] and "I Am a Prussian."[135]

Queen Auguste (called "Juste" by the people)[136] stepped out on her balcony. The crowd roared and shouted, "Long live the

---

[131] Sedan (September 1, 1870) was the decisive battle in the Franco–Prussian War. French emperor Napoleon III (1808–1873, nephew of Napoleon Bonaparte), had accompanied his troops to the front and was captured.

[132] Frederick the Great, king of Prussia 1740–1786.

[133] Sans Souci ("Carefree") in Potsdam, outside Berlin, was the palace of Frederick the Great.

[134] "Heil dir im Siegerkranz" became the unofficial national anthem of Imperial Germany (1871–1918).

[135] "Ich bin ein Preusse" (poem from 1830, set to music 1832) was the national anthem of the kingdom of Prussia; it remained popular in the German Empire.

[136] Queen Auguste was the consort of William I, king of Prussia, 1861–1871, and first emperor of Germany, 1871–1888. Note: in Berlin dialect, a "G" is pronounced like a "J" (sounds like "Y").

queen!" The queen gave a signal, and her adjutant came out and asked for silence. He held a paper in his hand and read from the dispatch that the queen had received from the king: "Divine Providence has brought about a wonderful turn of events."[137] At first, the crowd was completely silent. Then a few people began to sing the hymn "Praise Be to God on High; Let Us Thank Him for His Grace," and the whole crowd joined in. The queen called the sweep's boy up to her and presented him a golden cup for his efforts. Then the crowd began to drift away. Carl took me back to the store and later back home to the tents. Everywhere we went, there were people milling about, excited and happy and wondering what to do next. None of us really knew what to do. Everyone, old or young, rich or poor, tall or short, was overwhelmed by Prussia's victory.

---

[137] The Brandenburg Gate, decorated for Prussia's victory at Sedan, was hung with a banner bearing the phrase that Jenny quotes in her memoir: *"Welch' eine Wendung durch Gottes Fügung."*

THE FAMILY PROSPERS

Even before peace was made with France in 1871, we left the tent and moved in at 104 Leipzigerstrasse. Everything there had been remodeled. Running water! Now that was something! We no longer had to take barrels to the Royal Well to bring back water. A toilet! Gas lights! Gas chandeliers! No more messing with the oil funnel, although we kept a petroleum lamp here and there for reading and writing.

The flat had so much room that all of the uncles could live with us. Uncle Siegmund and Uncle Emmanuel also ate with us. Even before Uncle Siegmund came to live with us, he had taken an interest in me. I remember that when we lived on Behrenstrasse he would read Lessing's aphorisms and his play *Nathan the Wise* with me.[138] He would recite the play out loud and help me understand what we had read together. I really surprised Mama once when I was eight years old. I was sick with scarlet fever and asked her to bring me a copy of Chamisso's *Women's Love and Life*.[139] She was astounded when I began to recite "Ring on My Finger."

---

[138] Gotthold Ephraim Lessing (1729–1781), German classical writer. *Nathan the Wise*, his most famous play, has religious tolerance as theme. (Nathan, the main character, is a Jew.)

[139] Adelbert von Chamisso (1781–1838), French-born poet of the German Romantic period.

Between 1871 and 1873, Uncle Siegmund continued to familiarize me with German classical literature. We would choose parts and read plays aloud: *Minna von Barnhelm, Egmont, Don Carlos,* and *Wallenstein.*[140] No Shakespeare, unfortunately. It was not just that we read the plays aloud; it was also our conversations about plot and characters that helped me understand the works. Uncle Siegmund did not discourage me from expressing my own ideas. Sometimes he would take the opposing view, but he did not demand that I agree with him. Aesop's *Fables*, in Lessing's translation, provided fertile ground for our discussions.

In later years Uncle Siegmund's influence on me grew stronger. If he disapproved of something I said or did, he would chide me in a friendly and engaging way and explain why my words or behavior might hurt a person's feelings. He taught me how much variety exists in how people respond to things, and why people's personalities make them behave the way they do. He should have been a psychologist or an actor, rather than Uncle David's companion.

Uncle Siegmund's weakness was that he was almost too nice. He loved my sister, was proud of her beauty and jealous of anyone who danced with her, but he finally allowed himself to be trapped into marriage. It was a so-called "good marriage," but it wasn't right for him.[141] His wife was very pleasant, even-tempered, very rich, and well brought up and educated. But after

---

[140] Dramas by German classical authors Lessing, Goethe, and Schiller, respectively.

[141] Siegmund Simon-Meyer (or simply Meyer) married Hedwig Kosterlitz (1854–1932).

he married her, Uncle Siegmund became a different person. He ceased to be generous; his enthusiasm for beauty and culture fell dormant. He turned into a stodgy businessman, even though he had no special aptitude for that line of work. Later, on the rare occasions when I saw him alone, he would become warmer and more engaged, and would tell me what was on his mind and what his hopes were. But that was years later, if I ran into him on the street or somewhere in town. He would talk with me for an hour or so. We would walk together in the area around Sigismundstrasse,[142] and then he would once more be the same uncle I knew as a child.

After we moved to our flat on Leipzigerstrasse, we were closer to our grandparents, and we and Uncle Louis visited them more often than before. In addition, Uncle Julius, who had a store on the ground floor of our building, and Leser and Johanna and their children[143] would come to visit us. The children were about ten years younger than I was. Around this time I asked for and received private gymnastics lessons, because there was nothing like that at school. I really enjoyed those lessons.

That summer brought a pleasant surprise — a trip on the Rhein River! This took place because our doctor thought the trip would be good for Hanne's heart, which had been weakened by

---

[142] Sigismundstrasse is near the Potsdamer Platz, on the southern edge of the Tiergarten.

[143] Therese's sister Johanna or Anna (n.d.) married David Leser. They lived in Sondershausen. The only child for whom we have dates is son Siegfried (1872–1942).

her rheumatic fever. The waters in Wiesbaden[144] were said to be very beneficial. Papa usually went to Kissingen[145] for his annual cure, but was ready to try Wiesbaden. The day before Hanne and Papa were to leave, my parents decided that I should go along so that Hanne would have company. While I was taking my bath that night, Mama explained to me that I had a special task, which was never to let Hanne out of my sight. Oh, now I had the picture!

The train trip was at its most beautiful as we traveled around Marburg, the train climbing in circles.[146] In Wiesbaden we stayed about five weeks at the elegant Nassauer Hotel, where we took our mineral baths. We ate our midday meal at the hotel as well. Twenty-two years later Paula and James[147] visited the hotel, whose proprietress remembered us as cute young children and spoke of us and Papa. Right after lunch, if it wasn't raining, we would walk through the spa's garden and up to the Neroberg.[148] Hanne and I would have preferred to go to the garden more frequently to drink coffee and listen to the concerts, but we soon became aware that Papa didn't like sitting around; he always had to be on the move.

---

[144] Wiesbaden, the capital of the state of Hesse, is on the Rhine River across from Mainz, about 40 kilometers west of Frankfurt. Wiesbaden was famous for its mineral hot springs or "baths" (*Baden*).

[145] Kissingen is a spa town in the Bavarian region of Lower Franconia.

[146] Marburg is a university town in the state of Hesse.

[147] Jenny's younger half sister, Paula, married Berlin physician James Fraenkel (1859–1935).

[148] The Neroberg is an 80-meter hill just over a mile outside the center of Wiesbaden.

For a change of pace, Hanne and I would sometimes walk over to Biebrich.[149] We took a beautiful path through the forest. Hanne said to me: "Once, just once, Jenny, we have to have some fun, and at least watch the party from the outside, through the windows." We had made the acquaintance of a young Dutch girl, fifteen or sixteen years old, who wanted to watch the dancing too. She brought Hanne a pair of white gloves. It wasn't clear to me why Hanne needed white gloves if we were just planning to watch from outside. Dressed in our good summer dresses, we went walking for a while with our Dutch friend. Around eight o'clock in the evening we met the girl's mother. Everything seemed normal, until Hanne and the Dutch girl suddenly abandoned me, went into the ballroom and started to dance. I was left standing outside waving my hands, making signs to try to get their attention. We didn't get home until around half past nine, at the earliest. We only told Mama the whole story years later.

For years Hanne was not allowed to dance because of her rheumatic fever. Only when she was about twenty was she given permission to dance occasionally. But Hanne had an "I can do what I want" attitude, so she danced a lot and often. We had family dances once a week, Uncle Siegmund would give fancy balls, and we also had birthday balls, New Year's Eve dances and costume balls. Mama and I enjoyed hearing Hanne's reports after she had come home from a dance: who had flirted with her (to Uncle Siegmund's annoyance), how many times she had been asked to dance, how many corsages and flowers she had received.

---

[149] In Jenny's time, Biebrich was a village outside Wiesbaden; now it is inside the city.

I didn't understand why Hanne loved all this. She would tell me, "You avoid anything that's fun. The most you ever do is go to the Rothsteins' birthday parties, and then you wear just some old Sunday dress, never a pretty dance dress. You didn't even get dressed up for Max's doctorate party — when everybody who had a pair of legs was there, and all the women had on tailor-made ball gowns."

"But Hanne," I protested, "I did wear a fancy dress!"

My friend Mathilde Rothstein thought the same way I did. Mathilde, who could have had anything she wanted, placed no value on outward things. She was in the seventh class at school and had a fine character. She had one shortcoming, however: she possessed no youthful enthusiasm or idealism. I think she thought I was a pretty strange creature. But her friendship for me was sincere, and so were those of her brother Max and her sister Anna. Max and Anna were very gifted musically. Max was a wonderful pianist; I am grateful to him for taking Mathilde and me to the most sought-after concerts. Once we sat right behind the famous violinist Joachim[150] in the student section. The Rothstein household was a good one, one in which a child would be fortunate to grow up. Mathilde had diabetes for over forty years. This disease affected her personality, and she became more nervous. I last saw her ten or twelve years ago, Max perhaps seven.

Now, after this long digression, back to our trip on the Rhine. After Papa finished taking the waters in Wiesbaden, we took the

---

[150] Joseph Joachim (1831–1907), Hungarian-born Jewish violinist and composer, was the most famous European violinist of the second half of the nineteenth century. He was a close friend of Brahms.

ship down the Rhine to Cologne. Near Bingen, the ship stopped by the Lorelei Rock.[151] Naturally everyone sang the famous song: "I don't know what it means that I am so unhappy."[152] But in reality, everyone was quite happy indeed, holding a glass of Rhine wine as we cruised down the river, bathed in sunshine and surrounded by vineyards.

In Cologne I was more impressed by the wide double bridge than by the famous cathedral,[153] from which I nearly got thrown out. The choirboys in their red and white smocks, jumping around and waving their little incense pots, struck me as very funny. Papa was asked to please keep us quiet, and he immediately took us outside. I thus missed seeing the artwork inside this imposing structure. Papa interrupted our trip in Mainz, where we stopped to see his wine merchant. We visited enormous wine cellars where all varieties of wine were stored in casks taller than a grown man. We sampled the wines, and Papa ordered a barrel that was nearly as big as I was.

The following year we visited Aunt Hermine in Bad Wildungen.[154] I had not met her before. She was very pleasant and warm to all of us. Her husband, however, was uncultivated

---

[151] The Lorelei is a large rock outcropping on a dangerous bend in the Rhine River, and a high point of Rhine River cruises.

[152] The first stanza of *Lorelei* (1837), a famous ballad by German–Jewish poet Heinrich Heine (1797–1856), begins: "*Ich weiss nicht, was soll es bedeuten, dass ich so traurig bin.*" Heine left Germany and died in Paris.

[153] The cathedral in Cologne is the largest Gothic church in northern Europe. It was built over a period of more than six centuries (1248–1880). It survived World War II.

[154] Hermine, Therese's oldest sister, lived in Bad Wildungen, another spa town.

and not worthy of her. She had two daughters who were much younger than we were.[155] Neither daughter was as clever or refined as her mother, but we nevertheless liked Erna. I can hardly find the words to express what a wonderful woman Aunt Hermine was: courageous, self-sacrificing, tender, perceptive, a lover of beauty, a woman of high ideals who was at the same time a real workhorse. Her good sense came out in any situation, even though she lacked any formal education. She was one of the most outstanding people I have met in all my eighty years. All the Barth children loved her; whatever this aunt asked us to do, we did without question. Some years later her daughter Erna, when she was still unmarried, suffered from stomach ulcers and spent nine months with me in Berlin because her family was not able to provide her the diet she needed. Later she married and moved east,[156] and I moved to Hamburg.

We did not stay at Aunt Hermine's house during our visit to Bad Wildungen, but we went there to eat lunch. The guests amused me; I made up rhymes about them, and Mama and Aunt Hermine and Uncle Siegmund (who had arrived by now) laughed at my little poems. Bad Wildungen had a small castle on a hill in a park. It also had visitors who had come to take the cure, among them some officers. Hanne went to the fountain every morning to get mineral water for Mama, and proudly reported how many of the officers had introduced themselves to her. After that, Uncle Siegmund always went to the fountain with her. It was the same

---

[155] Erna and Betty, birth and death dates unknown.

[156] "East" is an imprecise term; it refers in general terms to the easternmost provinces or territories of the pre-1918 Empire.

story at the dances. On the way back we stopped in Kassel and visited the Wilhelmshöhe.[157]

Shortly after our return, Aunt Anna[158] came to visit again. She had some sort of kidney ailment that was being treated in Berlin. She loved novels and got a subscription to the Rosenberg Lending Library on Leipzigerstrasse, since our home library did not fulfill all her needs.[159] I was too young (eleven or twelve) to be allowed to read such stuff, but I was given the job of going to the library to exchange her books. On the way there and back I leafed through these modern books that my aunt would pick up and be unable to put down until she'd finished. Aunt Anna favored Hannchen and Paula over me, but she amused me so much that I didn't hold it against her.

Not long after Aunt Anna left, Uncle Siegmund came down with diphtheria and had to be quarantined. Alas, the quarantine wasn't effective and shortly before Christmas I also had to be Isolated because I had gotten diphtheria. Papa was afraid that he might come down with it too, and would barely stick his nose into my room once a day to ask how I was doing. I would shout: "I'm doing just fine!" Our old servant Marie was entrusted with the main nursing duties since she had already had the disease. Uncle Siegmund usually visited me in the evening; he would ask: "Can I bring you something you need?" I racked my brain but

---

[157] The Wilhelmshöhe in Kassel is one of the largest landscaped parks in Europe. Its Schlosspark is famous for the waterfalls that were incorporated into its design.

[158] Therese's sister Anna, wife of David Leser.

[159] There were many private lending libraries in Jenny's Berlin. Their members paid small fees for each book they checked out.

couldn't think of anything. But as Christmas grew closer I remembered that Mama had told me that she wanted a cloth to cover a little table with, so I asked Uncle Siegmund to bring me a cloth I could embroider. He brought me one, and I began to embroider it slowly and in secret. But soon I noticed that I was finishing the job unnaturally fast. When I asked Marie, she would say that my sick eyes just couldn't see the progress I was making. I later found out that Marie took the cloth and worked on it while I was sleeping; so much the better for my eyes, I suppose, and for the tablecloth too!

Around this time Hannchen decided she would elope with a tall blond American named Hilton.[160] She had met him at the home of grandmother's niece Polack. I could tell that Hanne liked him, but her infatuations were such regular occurrences that I didn't pay much attention. Our parents did not know the young man. As it turned out, Hanne confided in the housekeeper, and the housekeeper told my parents about her plan. I felt sorry for Hanne after they found out. For months after the frustrated elopement they treated her like a prisoner, and she had nothing to do except to sit home and sew, embroider and knit. That was terrible for her. She grew friendlier to me and read me letters that Hilton (and others!) had written to her, and had me transcribe them. I found it exciting because this adventure was real, and not one of Hanne's fairy tales.

Hannchen took a long time to get over this experience. Later she was courted by so many young men that she got bored with the whole thing. She finally married at the age of twenty-seven

---

[160] We have no other information about this "tall blond American."

because, as she said, "One has to get married eventually." It seems that the Barth children are capable of falling deeply in love only once. After that, the power of reason takes over. Once after Hanne's wedding we tried to count all her love interests; the number we came up with was forty-two, although two thirds of them weren't serious. After she got married, she fell in love just once again, but as she told me, "I thought about our mother and decided to stay in my three-year-old marriage."

Papa sold the house on Leipzigerstrasse after we had lived in it only a short time. That was a shame, because eight or ten years later the place was resold for three million marks. Papa bought a property at the corner of Grossbeerenstrasse and Halleschestrasse, and then with the help of Uncle Louis, who loaned him 15,000 marks, he bought a wonderful house on Potsdamerstrasse.[161] This house had a magnificent garden with cherry and other fruit trees, and there was plenty of space to put up other buildings. A famous sculptor later built a villa and studio there. Papa quickly began remodeling both the Grossbeerenstrasse and Potsdamerstrasse properties. It was a huge project because work had to be done on each of the twenty rooms — painting, plumbing, floor repair, and so on. Papa was in his element and Mama had an endless number of things to do.

---

[161] Israel is now investing in real estate. After German unification in 1871, the Berlin real estate market exploded; housing was at a premium. Israel caught this economic wave and became a rich man. By the time of his death in 1892, he is no longer a mere merchant, but a "*Rentier*" (landlord).

ADOLESCENCE, SCHOOL AND FRIENDS

I was in the second class now.[162] I complained a lot about headaches and had a "green" appearance. Dr. Rosenthal said that I was anemic, too thin and too nervous, and that I should stay out of school a year. "She can catch up later," said the doctor. "She must not read, but she can help with the household." My parents took his advice. I had to have an hour-long lukewarm bath every day, and I helped in the household so that the servants could keep up with the mess the painters and other artisans made. I learned how to cook. Papa once even praised a roast I had made, without knowing that I was the cook! One day I was asked to clean up a messy room on the ground floor. Under a pile of things, I found an odd book without a cover; its pages were crushed and it had a lot of pictures. I examined the captions. As soon as I realized what had fallen into my hands, I decided to hide it and read it. Nobody knew about my find. Mama would say: "Jenny is following instructions. She takes her bath every day and does everything she is supposed to. I have to praise her." Her praise made me uncomfortable, but how could I give up a big volume of Shakespeare without first reading it, knowing I

---

[162] The "second class" is the next-to-highest class in a *Höhere Schule* (secondary school). Jenny would now be about fourteen.

wouldn't get it back? I didn't tell even Hanne about this until many years later.

The months passed. Aunt Anna's children Leopold and Siegmund came for a few weeks. We had fun playing our old childhood games in the front garden and in the rooms of the house that hadn't yet been remodeled. We had become good friends during our visit to Sondershausen. My sister Paula must have been one or two when we went there.[163] On the second evening of our visit, we all went with Uncle Leser's relatives up to a place in the hills outside town. It was a little like the Kreuzberg[164] in Berlin: tables, benches, and things to drink. It was growing dark, and I was getting bored. I saw the heights in the distance and started on the path up to the enchantingly named Frauenberg.[165] I ran and ran, but the mountain did not get any closer. Sheet lightning began to flash all around me. I ran faster, and the path and the mountain seemed even more beautiful in the lightning. Then a true storm broke and it began to rain heavily. I couldn't go on, so I slowly turned back, my plan spoiled by the weather. After a while I began to hear voices calling out my name. It was Uncle Leser, his brother and several other people who were searching for me. They found me and took me to my mother, who had been fearing the worst. People brought up this

---

[163] Jenny has not previously mentioned this childhood visit to Sondershausen, which is a town south of Nordhausen (and not distant from Sandersleben). If Paula was a year old at the time, the visit would have taken place in 1868.

[164] Kreuzberg is a densely-populated and now largely immigrant district in Berlin. In Jenny's time, however, it was a rural space frequented by Berliners for weekend excursions and picnics. Small restaurants dotted the slopes of the 200-foot Kreuzberg ("Cross Mountain").

[165] Frauenberg: "Lady's Mountain," or "Our Lady's Mountain."

incident later to tease me, even after I was married. Years afterward I went up to the Frauenberg in a wagon with a big group of my friends. It was a disappointment, in the same way that the much-ballyhooed Kyffhäuser was.[166]

Uncle Leser was, in his own way, very much like my grandfather.[167] He was very pious. Behind his house he had built little lattice huts for the Sukkot holiday.[168] He closed his store on Saturday and strictly observed all the holidays and fast days. We children liked him for his kindness and his calm personality. Even my father, who did not observe any Jewish religious traditions at all, greatly admired him because he was the personification of virtue and loyalty. It was very nice in Sondershausen. We played outside a lot, and I enjoyed watching how my aunt dealt with her children and with her neighbors and relatives. Sometimes everyone was in perfect harmony; sometimes they were jealous and belligerent. None of this bothered the three Leser brothers; they knew that sunshine always follows a storm.

I had been away from school for nine or ten months when Dr. Rosenthal pronounced me well again. Mama had decided that all three of her children should learn a trade so that we could survive the hazards and reversals that life can bring. This was almost unheard of at that time in well-to-do German families, especially

---

[166] The Kyffhäuser Mountains are a low mountain range in northern Thuringia. Its tourist attractions include a huge ruined castle built during the reign of Frederick Barbarossa in the twelfth century.

[167] Grandfather Landsberger.

[168] Sukkot ("booths") is a Jewish festival, originally a harvest festival, celebrated in the fall. During the holiday, observant Jews often live and eat their meals outside, in a hut or booth built for the occasion.

Jewish ones. This sensible tactic was one that my mother's own life had taught her. I was to study so I could take the teaching examination.

Through his householders' association, Papa made the acquaintance of a teacher named Böhme who taught at the Queen Auguste School. My father liked the man, and they arranged for me to enter school in the second class. Böhme suggested that I should first have a month or two of tutoring from a teacher he recommended highly. She was Polish and was a Napoleon enthusiast. She was gentle, correct, and didn't crush me with too much homework. She showed my final essay to Böhme, who kept it (Mama told me). The topic of the essay was a phrase from Schiller: "The past is eternally silent."[169] I did not agree with Schiller at all, but notwithstanding my opinion, I was admitted to the second class; Böhme was the professor. At first I sat in the last row, but with time I moved forward. Uncle Siegmund helped me a lot with arithmetic. If he was not home in the evening, I would put my assignment and a pencil and paper on his bed. In the morning the paper, with the problems solved, would be lying outside the door for me.

By the time I got to be the first student on the third row, I sat by a lovely girl I called Keterschen, and I decided not to give up my seat. There were between forty and forty-three students in the class, and the air was musty and close. Whoever sat in the first seat on the third row could open the window and feel the fresh air before anyone else. After we finished two hours of classes, we had to go outside in the long courtyard. Here we could run

---

[169] Friedrich Schiller (1759–1805), German classical author.

around and eat while the other classes played circle games in another part of the yard. We were also allowed to chat during recesses. What a difference from the strict quiet of the Lenz School! When I returned to my seat, I tried to keep the window open as long as possible. Often the teacher had to ask me to close it. If I had to go to the front of the room to write or recite, I only stayed there as long as required, and went back to my seat by the window. Keterschen helped me with my arithmetic, and I helped her with French and gave her the answers in history and geography.

Three of us in the class were Jewish. I was a close friend of one of the others, Ida Jacob, who lived near us on Königgrätzstrasse. There was not a milligram of anti-Semitism in our class, neither in the students nor in the teachers. Our class was always united — from the slow and lazy ones all the way to the more gifted. Ida Jacob and I belonged to a clique of students who revered our history teacher, Herr Lange, who was about sixty. The members of our clique were among the best students in the class. First there was Mathilde Reuleaux, daughter of Professor Reuleaux.[170] Second was Ida Jacob, an incredibly diligent student. I was third. After us came Else Hamme, who was tolerated rather than accepted, and later Keterschen and Martha Schmiele, a hardworking, sensible and very nice girl. The last two and Ida Jacob were the only students who went on with me to the teachers' school, and with whom I stayed in contact after I married.

---

[170] Franz Reuleaux (1829–1905), a well-known engineer and mathematician.

As in the Lenz School, each of the students had a "class book" in which every teacher, at the end of the hour, wrote either a grade or a comment (the best grade was a four). At the end of the week, the head teacher looked at the books and would make it clear to us whether he was satisfied or displeased. In my case Herr Lange gave me a big smile. I was now in the first class, and was respected by my teachers. Lange lived near us on Königgrätzstrasse. If he was in the street and saw me walking to school in the morning, he would wait for me. We would walk to school together, talking about all kinds of things. I always had things I wanted him to explain. He was the only teacher who called me by my first name. (This was not at all common, and I was the only student with whom he did this.) He often asked me to bring one book or another from home for literature class, such as a collection of old Germanic poetry beginning with a translation of the Our Father, the Gudrun epic, the Niebelungs[171] and so on.

Once as we were walking to school, Herr Lange gave me a lecture about my attitude and behavior in Herr Rauch's English class. "It is clear that you want to upset him by not being prepared for class."

My reply, in so many words, was: "I don't like him and I don't like the way he teaches."

"But he has your best interests in mind. He wants to be sure that you don't end up as an elementary school teacher." I must have blushed at this.

---

[171] The Gudrun epic dates from the thirteenth century. The Niebelung stories came into German literature from Norse mythology; their characters later became the basis for operas by Richard Wagner.

Herr Lange stopped, put his hand on my shoulder and said sternly: "In the next teachers' meeting, I want to hear only good things about you." Then he walked on by himself.

In the next English class, Rauch asked who had prepared the Ossian[172] assignment. Since no one else responded, I did. He nodded to me, surprised. I translated the passage in nearly perfect verse form; it was a poetic translation. He nodded again when I finished. After that, we got along. Later after a school conference, Herr Lange repeated to me teasingly, "We should call her Genius, not Jenny." That remark made the rounds, since Rauch made it in other classes too. Later on several occasions he offered me positions in England as a teacher or governess. Although I wanted to go, Papa wouldn't allow it.

I was in the teacher preparatory course for two years, and passed the examination so I could teach in a high school for well-off girls ("as they were entitled," said Mama). On December 15, Mathilde Rothstein celebrated her birthday; that celebration fell in the midst of the exam period, so I came to the party in the same dress I wore to the examinations. Frau Rothstein told me, "You are the only person I know who has enough 'phlegm' to go to parties in the middle of examinations."[173] I was taken aback. But Max, who was standing beside her, smiled and said, "I thought you'd be here."

---

[172] The poetry of "Ossian," supposedly an ancient Scottish bard, was very popular during the Romantic period in literature, especially in Germany. These works appeared in the 1760s, allegedly "translated" by Scottish author James Macpherson (1736–1796).

[173] "Phlegm" means equanimity or self-possession.

The next year in early spring when the trees were in bloom, I would meet Martha Schmiele at six in the morning in the garden of our house on Potsdamerstrasse. We both loved Byron, and would sit translating "Manfred," "The Corsair," and most of "Childe Harold." Afterward I went to swimming lessons on Königgrätzstrasse. I kept up with my private swimming lessons for some years after that. During this time, I also became a member of the Lette Association,[174] where I went to listen to lectures on ethics given by Professor Paulsen from the University. I also heard lectures on literature by Dr. Wright. These two scholars had been appointed by Crown Princess Victoria herself,[175] who founded the Lette House. Its purpose was to provide education not only in the household arts of cooking, sewing, and the like, but in commercial trades also. The Lette House was something quite new and useful. Unfortunately the citizens did not thank her for it. Every day the princess's simple carriage would pull up in front of the school. She did not even have a fancy servant with her. She dressed simply. I could watch out the window each day as the Princess Royal of England arrived to inspect the institution she had created.

---

[174] The Lette Verein (Lette Association) was founded in 1866 by Prussian legislator and jurist Wilhelm Adolf Lette (1799–1868) to train young women in trades, crafts and commerce. Crown Princess Victoria was the association's patron and helped support it financially. The Lette Verein is still active in Berlin; it has five separate campuses devoted to educating women in fields such as computers and electronics, design, and pharmacy.

[175] Crown Princess Victoria (1840–1901) was the daughter of Queen Victoria of England and her consort Prince Albert. She married Prince Frederick William of Prussia (1831–1888). Frederick William became the second emperor of Germany as Frederick III in 1888, but died 99 days later.

One day when Frau Rothstein was visiting with Mama, she suggested that it would be nice if we three girls, Mathilde, Henni Strassman (daughter of the mayor of Berlin)[176] and I would take Italian lessons together. Nobody asked my opinion. Mama agreed and twice a week between three and four in the afternoon, even in summer, I had the pleasure of walking from the corner of Grossbeerenstrasse and Landsbergerstrasse to the lesson and back. The bus would have cost only five pfennings! Our teacher was quite acceptable. Mathilde was the best student of the three of us. After our lesson, we enjoyed visiting together and making music with Max. He played the piano, and I sang. Max was now studying cello. Sometimes Adolph would come too and we would play trios: Max on cello, Adolph on piano, and me singing the violin part. That was very funny. I had been taking singing lessons for a year. Then, alas, my voice changed and I had to give them up.

Hannchen had learned to play the piano quite well with her piano teacher Mietzke. I could play too, but only by ear; I learned many pieces by heart. My lessons with Mietzke did not last long because I made fun of him. I found him standing in front of a mirror in our living room, looking at himself. He asked me, "Don't I have a Junoesque figure?" When I burst out laughing, he slapped my face. I left the room without a word, went straight to Mama and told her I refused to take lessons from that man any longer. I was able to learn enough piano with my singing teacher

---

[176] Wolfgang Strassman (1821–1885), Berlin physician and politician. Jewish, and a leading proponent of Jewish assimilation. Member of the Berlin city council 1863–1885 and its president 1877–1885. Member of the *Fortschrittspartei* (Progressive Party) in the Prussian parliament 1879–1885.

to be able to accompany myself. My teacher even had me practice Chopin with him now and then.

In the meanwhile a lot had changed in our house. While we were still living on Leipzigerstrasse, or perhaps right after we moved to Grossbeerenstrasse, Uncle David married and left the house. His wife, Aunt Clärchen, was a beautiful and elegant woman. She had received an excellent education from her Polish grandmother, whom none of us liked. We were supposed to kiss her hand when we greeted her. That was something I wouldn't do! On the evening before the wedding, I had to recite a special poem written by Dr. Reich. I was dressed as a shepherdess (a reference to Uncle David's wool business). This was Uncle Siegmund's idea. I still remember the end of the poem: "May you sit in the wool — that is the shepherdess's wish for you."[177] This wish was richly fulfilled.

Uncle Siegmund loved costumes, disguises and surprises. I especially recall the New Year's Eve when Hanne was about fourteen and I somewhere between seven and nine. The celebration was to take place in Ernst Simon's restaurant on Unter den Linden Boulevard. The entire *mispoche*[178] was going to be there. Children, however, were excluded. Hanne and I were sitting dejectedly alone at home. We had never spent a New Year's Eve by ourselves. Not to be able to drink Papa's wine punch, crack jokes, or drop hot lead into cold water to learn one's fortune for the coming year — and no pancakes? Our parents had

---

[177] "*Mögt Ihr sitzen in der Wolle.*" Apparently an idiom meaning, "May you have lots of money."

[178] Yiddish word for relatives, often including fairly remote ones.

already left for the party when Uncle Siegmund came home to dress. He saw immediately how glum we were.

"Get dressed and come with me," he said.

"What should we wear? What will our parents say?"

"Just wear what you were wearing today — let's go!"

Once we were in the carriage he told us, "You are going to put on gypsy costumes, and at the party you'll tell your aunts' and uncles' fortunes for the New Year."

"That's wonderful, but what shall we say?"

So he told us what to say to each of them. We arrived at the costume shop, got dressed up and were given silk masks for our faces. Uncle Siegmund went into the banquet room first, and we came in five or ten minutes later. No one recognized us at first. We played our assigned roles very well. When I came to Mama to tell her fortune, she gave me her hand. The first word that popped out of my mouth was "Reschen,[179] you . . . ." Then I chuckled, and she grabbed my pigtail from behind and said, "Aha, I thought so." The other partygoers wanted to avail themselves of our fortune-telling skills too, so we told jokes and made predictions for everyone. They got even with us by making gruesome predictions for us in the New Year, but they also gave us all kinds of presents. Everyone had a wonderful time!

I cannot say enough about Uncle Siegmund's goodness and discernment. Our cousin Siegmund "the Black"[180] became the outstanding person that he was partly because of Uncle Siegmund's influence on him. Cousin Siegmund adored his uncle

---

[179] "Reschen" is a diminutive of Therese.

[180] Sicgmund Leser (1865–1935), son of Uncle David and Aunt Anna.

and did everything he could to emulate him. Uncle Siegmund's marriage was a great loss for us all. He wound up marrying against his will because of Aunt Clara's intrigues; in short, he found himself obliged to do the honorable thing. My parents were horrified and never went anywhere they thought they might meet Siegmund's parents-in-law.

Our relationships with our standoffish relatives eventually came to an open break. I was about fifteen years old and did not understand exactly what was going on. I had prepared a little play for the night of the wedding. When I asked the Rothsteins to play a couple of the roles, they rejected my offer out of hand. It wasn't really about the play — they were rejecting the whole idea of the marriage. Siegmund's wife was Aunt Clärchen's cousin. She was a passive, easily-satisfied person, but despite all the wealth she brought into the marriage, she was a miser. After marrying, Uncle Siegmund stopped being generous. They lost three children, but I think they only sorrowed over their last one, Hans. Uncle Siegmund became very depressed. Fortunately, he did not live long enough to see how his daughters turned out. The younger one married well (Dr. Leser), but wound up as a prostitute. And as for the older one — well, if Eduard Leser hadn't intervened, who knows what would have happened. I tell you this because there is a distinct coolness between me and that rich branch of the family. Hannchen and Paula get along with them better.

Mama's health had been deteriorating for some time. For the first six or eight years, her migraine headaches came every four or five weeks and lasted a day or less. Later they came more frequently and would last several days. These headaches were very hard on her. I think none of us really understood how much she suffered and how stoic she was. She went to all kinds of specialists, among them Dr. Jastrowitz, to seek advice. Some strange treatments were tried. I remember that they inserted a so-called "hair spindle" into her spinal canal, and that they laid a bandage filled with gold coins around her head and forehead. Those didn't help, nor did the cold compresses I placed on her head, just as the physician had prescribed, every morning before I went off to school. As time wore on, Mama's headaches got worse and became almost unbearable. In those days we lacked the pain-relieving medications we have now; perhaps they would have helped her. Still, even though she was sick, Mama kept on running the household and looking after her children. She even continued to entertain. Hanne, for example, would have her circle of friends over to our house. Some twenty to twenty-four friends and relatives would come to play forfeits,[181] make music and dance just as before. They dressed up in their best clothing to look elegant and attractive and (as we said then) "to cause a furor."

Among Hanne's friends was Bertchen Simon, who was a bit younger than the others. Our parents, Paula and I liked her a lot. She was gracious and willing to do a favor for anyone. She proved that to Paula, and I am grateful to her for that to this day. Unfortunately I was not able to return the favor. Bertchen's son died in the war in 1915, and she herself died all too young from cancer. Her oldest daughter got along well with Hanne.

---

[181] "Forfeits" is an old party game. In order to stay in the game (or in order not to lose an object one has pledged), the players are required to perform various silly tricks.

Unfortunately, when I moved to Hamburg I lost contact with almost all my relatives and friends in Berlin.[182]

---

[182] Jenny gave up her medical practice and moved to Hamburg about 1912, the year her son Arthur's wife Olga died, to manage the household and help raise Arthur's son Frederick (Fritz).

PHILIPP

annchen got engaged several years after Uncle
Siegmund's marriage. On April 27, 1879, we had the
first engagement-congratulations visit at our house.[183]
Many people came; the servants and I were busy for hours filling
wine glasses and serving cake. The whole show ended between
three and four in the afternoon, by which time Mama was worn
out and the rest of us were tired too. We ate a late lunch (already
warmed up more than once) and were having our soup when the
doorbell rang. We had all had enough of visiting, and nobody
wanted to answer the door. I stood up to tell the girl who was
serving at table to send any other visitors away, but instead
something else happened. When I opened the hall door, I saw a
tall, slim man standing with a hat in his hand, apparently
pondering something. He asked me if he could come in and
congratulate the happy couple and the parents. I answered that we
were all very tired and had just sat down to eat. His expression
became more earnest and questioning. I couldn't think of any
other way to ask him to leave, so at last I asked, "Would you
perhaps like to come in and wait for fifteen minutes?" He did not
answer, but his eyes, it seemed, were asking me what lay deep
down in my soul. I felt the same way I did when Professor Lange

---

[183] Jenny is now almost twenty years old.

would look at me, asking what I was thinking but didn't want to say. I could not answer. Finally the stranger said, "I'll come back in about an hour," and turned and left. I shut the door and walked pensively back into the dining room.

Mama's eyes are filled with loyalty and goodness. Father's eyes are dreaming of all the good things on earth (we called that his "babe in arms" look). But this man's eyes asked: "Who are you? All my life people have disappointed me."

I sat down at the table, occupied with these thoughts. Papa asked me, "Who was it?"

"I didn't catch the name."

"A man or a woman?"

"A man."

"He didn't tell you his name?"

"No."

"So you spent all that time and didn't find out who he was?"

Hanne's fiancé Wilhelm[184] asked me, "What did he look like?"

"Tall, slim, black hair, deep brown eyes, color in his face, mustache."

Wilhelm said, "That was probably my colleague Philipp Bornstein."

That startled me. So this was the man about whom Father had once said, "That fellow will never marry my daughter?" And why did he say that? Because Philipp had slammed the door to Father's private office as Father was going over the books and

---

[184] Wilhelm Bütow (1846–1926), Hanne's fiancé, was also an associate in Israel Barth's business.

telling his future son-in-law Wilhelm, "I can only give my daughter Johanna a dowry once." (Father told Mama this story in my presence.)

Once my surprise passed, it struck me (suddenly and not without a flash of willfulness) that Father would in fact wind up giving this man a daughter in marriage. I understood quite well why Philipp had slammed the door, and that he felt deeply offended that my father wouldn't accept his oral report on how the business was doing, but had to be shown in black and white. I was puzzled by only one thing. He had come to my father's house to offer his congratulations. That, of course, is the sort of thing an associate is expected to do. I had told him to go away, but he still wanted to come back. I will let one of his letters tell why he returned:

You ask me if I noticed the impression I made on you. Dear Jenny, out of the proud young man I used to be, I had become a prudent grown-up. To be honest, I was always somewhat reserved in the company of better-off Jewish families. Actually, I didn't like the atmosphere there very much. There the question was always, "What does this man have to offer? What accomplishments can he point to?" The question is never, "What kind of a man is he?" Often we are required to point to our accomplishments, when these accomplishments are not the ones by which we want to be measured. When I first saw you on the occasion of your sister's engagement celebration, I was amazed by the simple, modest dress you were wearing. And you wore your wonderful hair in such a simple, natural way that I had no idea I was dealing with the daughter of the house; I honestly thought you were a relative who was helping out for the occasion. I had no very high opinion of the modesty of the daughters of Israel. When you spoke to me, dear Jenny, I wasn't even able to reply; I held my hat in my hand and left without telling you my name. I went into a café and tried to read, but I couldn't concentrate. I kept thinking, who was that? Perhaps a sister of the bride-to-be? I knew we would become good friends. I knew that, and so decided to come back the same day so I could hear you speak. When I returned, I argued with you just to hear your voice. I heard you speak and knew immediately that your eyes and voice were speaking to me from your heart.

After dinner, Mama and Father went to take a nap. Hanne and Wilhelm were sitting in the music room. I was helping the servant girl clean up from the party and putting out dishes and cups for coffee later. I asked the servant girl to change her clothes and to answer the door if anyone should call. I was not overcome by curiosity or suspense. Rather, I knew someone would be coming, so I waited "phlegmatically," as Frau Rothstein would have said. Uncle Emmanuel was still living with us at that time. He and I were sitting comfortably together, reading the *Tante Voss*.[185] When the doorbell rang a little later, we kept on reading. The servant girl, as instructed, led the caller into the music room. Mama came in shortly afterward, much refreshed, followed by Papa.

Mama ordered coffee to be served, and opened the door to the music room. The stranger was introduced to her as Herr Bornstein (Papa already knew him well). She led him to the coffee table and introduced Paula as her youngest daughter, me

---

[185] The *Tante Voss* (Aunt Voss) that Jenny refers to is Germany's oldest newspaper, the *Vossische Zeitung*, which was published in Berlin from 1721 until 1934. It was generally considered Germany's national newspaper of record, much like *The Times* of London or *Le Temps* of Paris.

as her second daughter, and then Uncle Emmanuel. Herr Bornstein looked at me with a slightly confused expression. The table conversation was mostly about trade goods, manufacturers, and that kind of thing. The women barely spoke.

However, as we were finishing our coffee, the topic of conversation changed. Papa was talking about cloth manufacturing in Aachen. Philipp said, "I saw those factories in 1870; they made very good products."

Wilhelm asked, "Did you see them when you were in the army or were you traveling for Landsberger?"

"No, I saw them on the way to Verdun,"[186] said Philipp.

Then the conversation turned to 1870 and Papa and Philipp had a lively back-and-forth. Papa wanted to know Philipp's opinion about the strategies that were employed in the war, from A to Z. I was drawn into the conversation and contributed historical data. Papa was in his element. It quickly became clear that Philipp was a strong Bismarck supporter and Papa was a Richter progressive,[187] so that was a step forward. They were united in their love of country, in their support of German unification, and in their desire for the development of all of Germany's potential.

Mama, Uncle Emmanuel, Paula and the engaged couple had long since moved to another room because it appeared that the discussion at the coffee table was not going to end anytime soon. A little later Hannchen's girlfriends arrived: the Sonntag twins, Bertchen Simon, Auguste Sonntag and others. Mama called

---

[186] Verdun was the site of a battle in the Franco–Prussian war.

[187] Eugen Richter (1836–1906). Liberal lawyer, journalist and influential Reichstag deputy. A strong opponent of many of Bismarck's later policies.

Philipp into the room and introduced him all around. Papa smoked cigarettes and read. We made music and sang. Papa came into the room and asked Auguste Sonntag to sing the Schumann[188] duet for soprano and mezzo that he liked so much. Auguste and I sang and Auguste played the piano accompaniment: "How quickly springtime passes! Sweet springtime, gone so soon! One thing only makes me tremble: it is a longing that always passes. As soon as the dance music dies away, then amidst the yearning silence, love gives way to deepest sorrow, love becomes a yearning song." We had been planning to sing longer, but after this remarkable composition, I no longer had any desire to sing. Mama wanted to rest in the next room, so I went with her and arranged her pillows on the couch.

Then Philipp came into the room and asked if he could be of any help. He hoped his presence would not disturb Mama; he had heard many lovely things about her from his sister-in-law's family, and it was not likely he would soon have such a pleasant opportunity to visit with her again. He hoped it would not be too much for her to visit with him. I glanced at him disapprovingly because I knew that Mama needed her rest. He understood me immediately, and said, "I will visit with your daughter until you've had time to rest."

"I'm glad to listen to your conversation," replied Mama. "But won't the others in the next room miss you?"

"Oh no," said Philipp. "The engaged couple is much more interesting company than I am."

---

[188] The song may be "*Herbstlied*" ("Autumn Song") by Karl Klingemann (1798–1862), music by Felix Mendelssohn-Bartholdy (1809–1847).

Then we somehow got onto an awkward topic of conversation. Doris Walter was my classmate in the Auguste School[189] for a year and a half. All our classmates avoided her. She was very rich, friendly, good-natured, but a bit stupid. Her father was a known Jewish crook. As happens sometimes in Jewish families, everybody knew it except the children. For example, I was warned about my friend Martha W., "My angel, you say you want to visit her parents on Bellevuestrasse. You simply can't do that. If anyone sees you on the street with that family, your good name is gone forever." Despite that, I never gave up my friendship with Martha. She was an intelligent and warm-hearted socialist, and I am sad I never hear from her anymore. But to be friends with Doris Walter, who was so simple and childlike, just because she was Jewish?

As we talked, Philipp pressed me to be friends with her, but I wasn't old enough at the time to understand that I shouldn't blame a child for a parent's bad behavior. Besides, Doris never seemed to feel left out or to be upset over her bad grades or by the fact that teachers and classmates avoided her. Mores in old Prussia were quite different from those of today. Today people don't ask where or how someone made his money; the only question is how much money he's got.

I was trying to stay away from controversial topics as we talked. But despite my desire to avoid stating unpleasant facts, it seemed the conversation kept coming back to the Jewish female and Jewish characteristics, and this being the main factor in how

---

[189] The Auguste School (Augustaschule) was the secondary school in which Jenny enrolled at about age fourteen after she recovered from her adolescent illness.

the teachers and students felt about Doris. Philipp would counter my arguments and try to pin me into a corner, until I finally just decided to put my cards on the table.

"As far as I am concerned there is no Jewish belief in the way you understand it."

"But Jenny!" cried Mama.

"Nor in any other way, either," I continued. "I am a socialist;[190] all men are brothers — don't you listen to Beethoven?"[191]

I kept pushing my argument. "I go farther than Jesus, whom I revere; I agree with Nietzsche, who said: 'I love others even more than myself when they are in need or seek help.' Moses gave us good, eternal laws, but most of the time they are not felt in their deepest sense. Jesus felt them. Who else felt them with such purity? Perhaps the ancient Asians, who speak of them in their pandects."[192]

Mama looked at me in total shock. Philipp didn't say anything, but I saw a twinkle in his eyes.

---

[190] Although a banned Socialist Party existed in Germany in 1879, the Social Democratic Party of Germany (SPD) was not founded until 1890. Jenny states in a footnote that she later attended sessions of the Reichstag at which Socialist Party deputies introduced legislation. German women, however, did not have the legal right to join political parties or attend political meetings until 1908; they gained the right to vote only in 1919. Jenny's actual political participation is unknown.

[191] Jenny is quoting from the lyrics of the last (choral) movement of Beethoven's Ninth Symphony.

[192] The term "pandect" means a compendium of laws, but Jenny is probably using it to refer to the teachings and canons of Eastern religions generally.

I knew Philipp had been raised an orthodox Jew, but in truth he was a socialist in the best sense of the word. We continued talking for a long time, until it was announced that it was time for dinner.

Philipp looked at his watch and said, "Today is my birthday and my brother and his family have a dinner planned for me tonight. I'm so sorry I have to leave. Might I call again another time?"

The second time Philipp and I met was about a month later. It was a Sunday afternoon around four o'clock. I was sitting at a table in the piano room. My parents were asleep. The engaged couple was out making return visits. I had no idea anyone would be visiting and was translating Dante's *Divine Comedy* for tomorrow's lesson. The doorbell rang. The maid peeked into the room and asked me what she should say. Without thinking I said, "If you know the person, ask them to come in." A moment later, Philipp Bornstein walked into the room. I put my finger to my mouth and pointed to a chair facing me. He sat down, looking a bit embarrassed. I said softly, "Mama has a migraine and Papa is taking his midday nap. The engaged couple will be back around five o'clock."

"Am I disturbing you?" he asked.

"No," I said. "Perhaps you might be interested in one of the books on the table?"

"What are you reading?"

"I'm translating a chapter from Dante's *Divine Comedy*."

We started to talk about Dante's work.

Then Philipp said, "My friend Fürst has a German translation. I'll bring it to you; it will save you a lot of trouble."

I said no thank you but he insisted, saying it was a good translation, or so it had seemed so to him when he read it. Then he picked up an edition of *Fridtjof's Saga*,[193] a work he really loved, and told me that despite his Jewish beliefs, he knew no finer verse than the one he wanted to read to me. He leafed through the book until he found the right passage, and handed the book to me.

"Take this rune — the human heart is the greatest wonder of all."

We sat in silence for five or ten minutes. Then the engaged couple arrived home and walked into the room. I got up quickly and broke away from what remained unspoken but had nonetheless taken place, and went to get coffee and cake. We did not exchange another word that day.

At the table, Herr Bornstein told my parents he was going to Dresden in a few days, and asked them if he should take a look at the sanatorium in Königsbrunn.[194] They gladly accepted his offer, because they had been thinking of this sanatorium for Mama's summer cure. The next day an apprentice from B & B's store[195] brought me the German translation of Dante's *Divine Comedy*. About a week later, my parents received a message from Philipp

---

[193] *Fridtjof's Saga* (1825) was a romantic epic poem by Swedish writer, professor and bishop Esaias Tegner (1782–1846). It was the most widely read work of Swedish literature in the nineteenth century, and was translated multiple times into German.

[194] This Königsbrunn, in Saxony, was a spa and sanatorium near Königstein. It should not be confused with the town of Königsbrunn south of Augsburg in Bavaria.

[195] "B & B" perhaps stands for "Barth and Bornstein," or perhaps for "Barth and Bütow."

saying that he thought Königsbrunn was a fine place for a cure because it offered plenty of quiet, lots of fresh air, and lovely places to walk.

Around this time Grandfather fell ill with a stomach disorder. Was it cancer? I can see him standing by the window on the Dönhoffplatz, gazing at the tall trees outside and murmuring, "The tree, the tree." I imagine he was identifying himself with the tree and thinking, "You too were once that tall and strong." Twenty-two years earlier he had also fallen ill with a stomach problem. No one could cure him. At last he consulted a naturopath,[196] Dr. Sorge (Paula and Dr. Sorge's daughter were good friends). Dr. Sorge cured him. Now that he was sick again and all the doctors had given him up, he went back to Dr. Sorge. After examining him, Dr. Sorge told Grandfather, "There is nothing I can do for you. You'll have to live with your pain."

Grandfather refused to take pain medications; "Man must accept what Jehovah wills," he said. Grandmother could not change his mind. While he still lived, he obeyed all the commandments and said his prayers as always. Two weeks before his death, he was no longer able to get out of bed. I stayed with Grandmother those entire two weeks as well as a few days after the funeral. Then Grandmother asked her niece to come stay with her, and she turned on me and Hanne the same way she had turned on my dear mother. She was the sole heiress of the estate. She later gave away much of her inheritance to her nieces, brother and nephews. The Dresden Jewish Welfare Committee, having heard about this, went to her and made her contribute

---

[196] A branch of medicine that believes in the self-healing power of the body.

15,000 marks for the care of the Hirschberg children.[197] Hanne and I were very happy to hear about that, but Papa said scornfully, "Should I demand 15,000 for you both as well?" Hanne and I were speechless and just shook our heads. How disgusting it seemed to fight over money!

---

[197] The Hirschberg children were Bella's younger children and Jenny's half brothers and sisters. This is the only time Jenny mentions the name of Bella's second husband.

INTERLUDE IN SAXONY

Mama was now in Königsbrunn. Paula, like all children, was on vacation in July. Then we received an invitation from Frau Rothstein for Paula and me to go with her and her children to visit Mama in the "Saxon Switzerland." We accepted with delight. In the third class carriage, I took the black flower off my mourning hat[198] and placed a slender moss-green ribbon around it. Frau Rothstein was amazed at how this "phlegmatic" young lady carried off that stroke of fashion! She didn't know that my trick was to use the hat as the final touch to make an outfit stand out. Mama recognized my talent at this, as well as in doing her and Hanne's hair.

Mama greeted us with great joy. We had a wonderful time together. We children loved everything about the place, especially our evening walks along the stream, with its rocks glistening in the moonlight. As we walked, Max Rothstein told me about his goal of a university career, about which we were both enthusiastic.[199] He wanted to be a professor with many students; I could envision him as a decipherer of ancient inscriptions and documents. Such are one's dreams.

---

[198] Jenny is wearing mourning for her just-deceased grandfather.

[199] Max Rothstein in fact became a Classics (Latin) scholar.

The high point of our trip was our hike through the "Saxon Switzerland." Max and Anna and I and two boys aged six or nine (far too young) hiked over Little Winterberg and Big Winterberg to the Trevishtor. Everything was delightful, although we lost our way and had to persuade the young men to stop and rest now and then. Max insisted that we eat grilled chicken at the Trevishtor. First the chickens had to be killed, then they had to be cooked. That took quite some time. In the meantime, the sky grew darker. When Max heard the first rumbles of the approaching storm, he suggested we break off the hike and go home. Not I! I wanted to see the lightning on the mountains and in the forest. Max was absolutely horrified. But I foolishly didn't want to miss the thunder and lightning. But once the treetops began to rustle and shake and I saw lightning and heard the thunder booming, I was "satisfied," and ran with the others downhill through the woods amid bursts of rain. It was late when we rejoined our parents and the other children. But it was a wonderful show.

When the Rothsteins went back to Berlin, I stayed behind with Mama (Paula did too, if I remember correctly). Mama seemed sufficiently reinvigorated by now for us to visit the Edmundsgrund as well as Tetschen and its remarkable castle park.[200] The park was filled with statuary figures from Greek mythology, including two or three of Zeus, plus all the other gods and goddesses and discus throwers and heroes. When I had finished answering all Mama's questions about the statues, I noticed that a number of other visitors had been following us around; Mama found that amusing. One man raised his hat and

---

[200] Tetschen is now Decin, in the Czech Republic.

came over to her. He excused himself and the others, saying: "We were charmed by your daughter's voice. We hardly ever hear such a wonderful delivery, even on the stage." The gentleman was Austrian. I'm sure it was my enthusiasm for the Classical statues (the Classics were my ideal) that had launched me into the declamatory mode.

I think Mama stayed in Tetschen until Paula's vacation ended. We returned home and learned that Aunt Gertrude would be Hanne and Wilhelm's *dame d'honneur*. One evening Hanne, Wilhelm and I went to Frerichs's restaurant. There we ran into Philipp Bornstein and his brother, who was a grass widower that evening.[201] The three men talked business. Philipp sat the farthest from me, at the end of the long table. Hanne and I talked among ourselves and didn't take part in the men's conversation. After about an hour and a half, a flower girl came over to our table with a basket of violets. Wilhelm didn't want to buy any, but Philipp selected two small bouquets. He came over to me, put one in my hand and asked softly if he could pin the other on my jacket.

I said, "That bouquet wasn't for my sister?"

Without a word, he pinned the bouquet to the middle buttonhole on my jacket.

After a while the group broke up. Philipp and I walked together toward the Leipzigerplatz. We talked about Mama's health and Königsbrunn. I told him the story about the storm. He looked at me, shocked.

"Don't you know that storms in the forest can be deadly?"

---

[201] *Strohwitwer*, meaning a husband whose wife is out of town or elsewhere. We have no additional information on Philipp's brother.

"Yes," I replied.

"And you did it anyway? Weren't you thinking of your parents and — of me?"

At that moment we reached the Leipzigerplatz. Fortunately our friends were there, so I was spared from answering his question.

As I fell asleep that night, two adventures I had just had in Königsbrunn were running through my mind because I *was* thinking about him. Only Uncle David knew about them; fortunately he had been discreet enough not to say anything.

One of these dramas had taken place when Mama, to my great surprise, had decided to join a group that was going up to the Lilienstein, located across from the Königstein.[202] The Elbe River, navigable at this point, flows between the two mountains. Herr Hauptmann[203] was carrying Mama's coat and purse, and Mama and I were climbing slowly up the slope behind him. Mama was quite taken with Herr Hauptmann's attentions and courtesies, but I did not care for him. I could have carried Mama's things, but then I wouldn't have been able to hold her arm and support her as we climbed. After we had climbed about two hundred meters, we reached the first restaurant. Mama decided to stay there and knit. An older man who had also gotten tired from the climb stayed to keep her company. Herr Hauptmann and I continued up the mountain, whose heights the other members of our party had already reached. At first he and I talked about the scenery and the beautiful view, but suddenly he

---

[202] The Lilienstein and the Königstein are hills outside Königsbrunn.

[203] Jenny gives no other information about Herr Hauptmann.

began to complain about how lonely he was, living by himself in Dresden, and that I, of all the people in the world, was the woman he needed in his life. Barely had those words left his mouth than I ran on up the mountain alone. Herr Herz, a member of our party, saw me scrambling up and thought that perhaps something had happened to Mama. But when he heard and looked at me closely, he realized that the problem had nothing to do with Mama. He accompanied me up to the peak to join the others. I knew Herr Herz well because he had often walked with me when I went to buy medicine or other things for Mama. The path we took followed the edge of the forest, opposite a chain of little hills. It was a seldom-used path through the valley, a little less than an hour outside Königsbrunn. As we walked, we would chatter about excursions, the Dresden Royal Theater or boat trips on the Elbe. For my part, I would tell him about Berlin. Our party did not spend much time up on the Lilienstein, which was fine with me. At last we all came down the mountain, found Mama, and ate lunch together. In the meantime Herr Hauptmann had disappeared.

Then on the following day Uncle David came to visit us. Mama and I were delighted, and enjoyed his company for two days. Uncle David was surprised to find Herr Herz there, and told us he was a salesman for Herr Herz's woolens products. The next morning when I went out to the arbor, I was surprised to find Uncle David already there, the breakfast table set for two. Uncle David had arranged for the two of us to have our coffee together. Mama had stayed in bed to drink hers. After finishing breakfast, we had the following conversation.

"So, you've become friends with that nice fellow, Herr Herz?" he asked.

"Well, that would be exaggerating, Uncle."

"He thinks you like him quite a bit."

"I must say that I think he is a good-natured and sincere gentleman."

"He tells me that he likes you very much and would do whatever it would take to make you happy. If you would be his, he would provide you a secure life and fulfill all your wishes."

"Oh, Uncle," I said, "this new role of yours doesn't suit you at all. Can't we talk about something else?"

"Jenny, don't be childish," said Uncle David. "An honorable gentleman is courting you, he loves you, and he is very rich. He and his brother have one of the best wool-spinning factories in the country. He has a villa and owns half of Dresden. A carriage would always be at your disposal, you would have your own box at the opera and at the theater, and you'd even have your own riding horses. You could visit Berlin to see your parents as often as you want. You could invite them to visit you or even to live with you. His villa is spacious and beautifully furnished. Jenny, think it over before you say no. Your parents would be very happy if you were to say yes to his proposal. Can't I please ask Herr Herz to wait for your answer for a day or two? Young girls often need a little time to comprehend their good fortune."

"Dear Uncle David," I said, "I do not need all those things to make me happy. It just doesn't appeal to me."

"Well then," said Uncle David, "what does appeal to you?"

"I have a hard time explaining that," I said. "It's just that you and I have a different idea of happiness."

"Would you prefer to marry Max Rothstein? Aren't the two of you close?"

"No, I like him as a friend, but not to marry."

Then Uncle David asked me straight out, "Are you in love with somebody else?"

"Yes," I said.

"Are your parents aware of this?"

"No."

"Why not?"

"They need to get to know him better."

"Well," sighed Uncle David, "then I'm wasting my time. It's a shame; I feel sorry for Herr Herz."

"So do I," I said, "but I can't do anything about it."

That same day in the evening, Herr Herz left Königsbrunn. Ten or twelve years ago I read his obituary in the German newspapers. Other people took over his factory. I knew a young lady from Hamburg who had moved to Dresden after she married. She told me about Herr Herz and said that he had always been interested in what I was doing.

Uncle David didn't say anything to Mama and Papa. That was a well-considered and considerate decision on his part. He never brought up Herr Herz again, even when I experienced my great sorrow.[204] He never once said "what if" or "if only," and he was loyal and supportive to me. When I began to practice medicine, I became the physician for all the women in Uncle David's family. It took up a lot of my time, but at that point they were all very devoted to me. I continued caring for them for several years after Uncle David's death, but one day Aunt Clara[205] asked me, "You liked Uncle David better than Uncle Siegmund, didn't you?"

---

[204] Jenny is alluding to Philipp's early death (1891).
[205] Uncle David's widow.

I told her truthfully, "No, Auntie, I always liked Uncle Siegmund better."

She got very angry and said some very harsh things to me. In years to come, she wouldn't let me visit her and said ugly things about me behind my back. She and her children broke off relations with me. Even Heilchen Meyer, Aunt Clara's cousin and sister-in-law, stopped speaking to me. Some people just don't like to hear the truth.

ENGAGED

Before my engagement to Philipp, I saw him not more than four times. On two of those occasions my parents were present. Once Mama tried to explain my unusual tastes and point of view to Philipp. Only one thing surprised him and made him uncomfortable: "Jenny is not a good money manager." Those were Mama's exact words. I was amazed when I learned about this; Mama must have forgotten, or just not have paid attention to what I did with my little bit of money. Philipp did not say a word in reply, but when we had been married about a year, he came home after finishing the annual inventory at the store. He whispered in my ear, "You do know how to spend money wisely. I was happy to find," he said, "that we spent only half the money that Bütow did, even with our trip to Switzerland and our cultural activities. But what is really amusing is that, even before the wedding, I knew exactly how you spent your money and that you didn't lack for anything."

On December 14 or 15, 1879, Papa and I were invited to celebrate Wilhelm's birthday. I only went because Frau Rothstein stayed with Mama in the evening. Papa came along a bit later so that he could bring me home. I was surprised to meet Philipp at the celebration. He had just returned from Bentschen,[206] where he had visited his seventy-four-year-old mother. Papa was listening as Philipp talked about his family home and the way Jews lived in that Polish-speaking part of Germany. The two of them spontaneously exchanged a few words in Polish, which I did not understand, so I went over to sit by Hannchen. Later I learned that Papa had invited Philipp to visit us some Friday evening.[207]

On Friday December 19, 1879, the Bütows came to dinner. I had to add another place setting because Herr Bornstein was coming as well. I was surprised that Philipp had taken up Papa's invitation with such alacrity. I did not take part in the dinner conversation, and didn't go to Mama's room with her after dinner. Instead I visited with Paula or worked in the kitchen. I was nervous and a bit annoyed. As I was putting the good dishes away in the buffet, the door opened and Philipp came over to me saying, "When the heart is full, it's hard for the mouth to speak. For months I have been amazed at the skill with which you've made me speechless, but tonight you can't avoid me. I am not Fridtjof, but I love the same way Fridtjof loved. Do I have to sail the seas first, or shall we walk life's path together?"

"Well," I said, "if you truly feel that way, and are sure I am the woman who will make you happy, and always will be . . . ."

---

[206] Bentschen (now Zbaszyn) is a town in the eastern province of Posen (now in Poland).

[207] The Jewish Sabbath begins at sundown on Friday. It is usually celebrated with dinner in the home. By inviting Philipp to take part in this family event (perhaps also by making the invitation in Polish), Israel is likely signaling his approval of Philipp's courtship of Jenny.

He embraced me then. Hannchen walked into the room, turned around and left immediately.

Philipp clasped my hand and said, "I know you are the woman I always longed for and never thought I would find. To me you mean all the happiness the world has to offer. Let's go to your parents. I have to write my mother immediately, too. I've already told her about you, and she has probably been praying for us both ever since. If we write to her right away, she'll get our letter tomorrow."

Then he asked, "Can you write Hebrew?"

"No," I said, "but I can learn it in a day."

And that's what happened. Papa showed me how to do it. [208]

Later that evening I woke my sister Paula, who was already asleep. "Paula, Paula, I'm engaged!"

She was sleeping so soundly that the only thing she could manage to mutter was: "What for?" Then she turned over and went back to sleep.

At first I was amused by her question, but later when I was trying to fall asleep I asked myself rationally (recalling that Frau Rothstein had once called me "phlegmatic"), "Why have you agreed to this? Don't you have a nice life with your parents? Don't your parents and sisters love you? Don't you have good friends? Aren't you free to study and think and do what you want? Do you really have any wishes that can't be fulfilled?" As I asked myself these things, I began thinking about my dear

---

[208] Philipp and Jenny are not talking about writing in the Hebrew language, but rather about writing the German language in Hebrew characters. Central and Eastern European Jews first learned to read and write in Hebrew, and it was common for them to write the vernacular language in Hebrew script.

mother and the terrible fate her marriage had led her to. What for? What for, indeed?

I asked myself, "Couldn't you be satisfied to have him remain just a good friend who is compatible with you?" But his eyes had spoken to me about being lost, homeless and joyless. Did they make me feel as compassionate as Desdemona?[209] No, his eyes, his bearing, told me clearly and conclusively, "I am a fighter, and hopefully your helper." Then, deep inside me, I knew the answer to Paula's question, What for? Because I want to be united to him and see his eyes shine with as much happiness as mine do now in joyous anticipation.

It must have been about half past seven in the morning of December 20, 1879, when I felt someone shaking me awake. My dear mama was standing next to my bed. At first I was surprised; had I forgotten to do something?

"No," she said, "I just wanted to see your face."

I laughed and pointed at the clear winter sun shining into the room. "Mama, the sun is smiling at me." And for eight full wonderful years the warm sun shone down golden . . . . [210]

---

[209] In Shakespeare's *Othello*, Desdemona is Othello's loving and innocent wife (he murders her out of jealousy).
[210] The rest of the sentence is illegible.

PART III

EPILOGUE – JENNY'S LATER LIFE AND DESCENDANTS

At the end of 1879, Jenny's life was only beginning. She and Philipp married in 1880. In the following eight years she gave birth to three children: Arthur (1881), Therese, also known as Rose (1885), and Suzanne (1888). Jenny's stepmother, Therese, died July 21, 1881. Jenny's sister Paula writes that Therese had made it clear she wanted an autopsy performed so that others could benefit from the diagnosis of her illness.[211] This wish could not be fulfilled because Therese died in midsummer, when all the physicians competent to do the autopsy were away from Berlin on vacation. The widowed Israel Barth continued to live in his large house on Grossbeerenstrasse until his death in 1892. Jenny, Philipp and their growing family lived in their own flat in the same building. By the time Jenny's first child Arthur was a pupil in elementary school (1886 or 1887), Israel was living at home from the income of his successful real estate investments. Arthur recalls coming home from school and visiting his grandfather, who would give him a gold coin for his good grades.[212]

---

[211] Unpublished memoir of Paula Barth Bütow (1937).
[212] Unpublished juvenile memoir of Arthur Bornstein (perhaps 1897).

By the late 1880s Philipp Bornstein was seriously ill, reportedly from an illness contracted during his military service in Prussia's wars of the 1860s.[213] Travel to health resorts, spa treatments, and months spent in the healthy air of the Harz Mountains did not slow the progression of his disease.[214] A year or more before his death he was interned in the Berlin sanatorium founded and operated by neurologist Dr. James Fraenkel, who became his physician. Jenny must have spent many hours at the sanatorium helping care for him. Arthur states that she also tutored students to earn money while Philipp was hospitalized. An unanticipated result of Philipp's extended hospitalization was that Jenny's sister Paula met and fell in love with Dr. Fraenkel. Philipp's death in December 1891 was shortly followed by that of Israel Barth, in March 1892. Paula and Fraenkel married in 1892, not long after Israel's death.

The deaths of Philipp and Israel, we believe, left Jenny a financially self-sufficient widow. We have no indication that she contemplated marrying again. There was no economic reason for her to do so, and she was already the mother of three children. Jenny turned thirty-three in July 1892. In 1893 she moved with her children to Switzerland and entered the medical school of the University of Zurich. Swiss medical schools offered the opportunity to study medicine to women who could not do so in

---

[213] Philipp's Prussian service record shows that he served in the 1864 war against Denmark, the 1866 war against Austria, and the Franco–Prussian war of 1870–1871. In the last of these wars he served as a non-commissioned officer (Jews were still barred from the officer corps at the time).

[214] We do not know the diagnosis of Philipp's fatal disease. Meningitis is a strong possibility.

their own countries, especially women from Germany, whose universities were closed to women until 1908, and from Russia, where medical school slots for women (especially Jewish women) were limited.[215] Jenny received her M.D. degree in 1898, having written a doctoral dissertation titled "A Case of Interstitial Myocarditis."[216] Licensed in Switzerland, she nevertheless returned to Berlin, where her son Arthur began his own medical studies.

Jenny did not leave us a written explanation of her decision to study medicine. At the time, her decision was exceptional and audacious, because the German medical profession was closed to women. It is plausible that the illnesses and deaths of her parents and husband inclined her toward medicine. Jenny also possessed a strong social conscience, evident in her memoir, and may have had a desire to bring medical help to Berlin's underserved poor. And the influence of Dr. James Fraenkel, now married to Paula, may have been crucial. Still, we cannot know with certainty what drove Jenny to uproot herself from Berlin and begin the ambitious project of remaking herself as a physician.

After she her returned from Switzerland, Jenny served as house doctor for a merchants' and tradesman's association, providing medical services for its female members.[217] As she tells in her memoir, she also served as physician to the women of her

---

[215] Bonner, Thomas N. "Pioneering in Women's Medical Education in the Swiss Universities, 1864–1914," *Gesnerus (Swiss Journal for the History of Medicine and Sciences)*, no. 45 (1988), pp. 461–74.

[216] Bleker, Johanna and Sabine Schleiermacher, *Ärztinnen aus dem Kaiserreich: Lebensläufe einer Generation* (Weinheim: Deutsche Studien Verlag, 2000), p. 238.

[217] Bleker and Schleiermacher, *Ärztinnen*, p. 238.

Uncle David's family. Germany first allowed women to sit for state medical licensing examinations in 1901; the next year, Jenny passed the state examination at the University of Marburg and was licensed as a physician.[218] She then practiced medicine in Berlin until 1912; her main area of practice was gynecology and obstetrics.

For his part, Jenny's son Arthur received his M.D. from the University of Kiel in 1903. Not later than 1908 he married Olga Brunstein, a Russian national from a Jewish family in Odessa, who had received her M.D. from the University of Geneva in 1901. Arthur and Olga (also known as Adele) first lived and practiced in Berlin; Arthur later held an appointment in Göttingen. The couple moved to Hamburg in January 1909 when Arthur was named project doctor for the Elbe Tunnel construction project. This was a huge civil engineering project that connected Hamburg's harbor to the workingmen's quarter of St. Pauli upon its completion in 1911. "Caisson sickness," also known as the bends, was a serious medical threat to the project's workers. Arthur and Olga/Adele carried out experiments in high-pressure medicine and wrote and published together from 1909 to 1911.[219]

Olga/Adele died of cancer in January 1912, leaving Arthur with a two-year-old son, Frederick. Fortunately for Arthur's medical career, Jenny soon moved to Hamburg to help manage

---

[218] According to family legend, Jenny scored higher on the licensing examination than Arthur did. This is unconfirmed.

[219] *See* Faesecke, Karl-Peter, *Ein Pressluftarzt für Hamburg: die medizinischen Forschungsarbeiten von Arthur and Adele Bornstein beim Bau des ersten Hamburger Elbtunnels 1909–1910* (Kiel: Edition Trident, 1998).

his household and to take charge of Frederick's care. (Arthur, in his juvenile memoir, had already noted Jenny's "nearly pathological sense of duty.") Even though Jenny was then only fifty-three, she did not practice medicine again. Although it is perplexing that Jenny would abandon the career she had begun only twenty years earlier, we have to conclude that Jenny's sense of family duty outweighed her devotion to the practice of medicine.

Jenny took charge of Arthur's household during the First World War (1914–1918), most of which Arthur spent in military service as an army physician on both the western and the eastern fronts (he received the Iron Cross, First Class). Arthur continued to rise in his profession after the war ended. He became a professor of physiology and pharmacology at the University of Hamburg and served as the dean of its medical school. He also headed a prestigious research laboratory housed in Hamburg's Sankt Georg Hospital [220] He died of heart disease in January 1932.

We have far less information about Jenny's two other children, Therese/Rose and Suzanne. We know that Therese/Rose married Olga Brunstein's brother Wolodya, but we do not know when or where. Therese/Rose and Wolodya lived for some years in Berlin before they left Germany with their two children Ilse and Emmanuel for the Soviet Union (probably after 1933). They

---

[220] In 1925 the Swedish Nobel Committee for Physiology and Medicine invited Arthur to submit a proposal for their consideration in selecting the recipient of the 1926 prize in Physiology and Medicine. We do not know if Arthur replied; the 1926 prize was awarded to Johannes Fibiger, a Dane.

took up residence in Leningrad, but disappeared during Stalin's purges of the mid-1930s.[221]

Jenny's daughter Suzanne became a social worker and was employed by the Berlin police department. She did not marry. She emigrated to Palestine after the Nazis came to power, and was living there when Jenny arrived in 1935. Suzanne either lost or was swindled out of the money she brought with her from Germany, and thereafter lived a hand-to-mouth existence until she died in Israel in the 1950s. Suzanne had no children. We have no indication that the relationship between Jenny and Suzanne was either close or happy.

When the Nazi dictatorship came to power in January 1933, it quickly passed sweeping anti-Jewish legislation and began the active persecution of Jews. Jenny left Germany for Palestine in April 1935. Neither of her two living children remained in Germany, and her grandson Frederick[222] had left Germany for the United States in 1934 after completing his medical education. Jenny remained in Palestine for two years; in 1937 she was able join Frederick and his wife Clara in the small central Illinois town of Rochester, near Springfield. Frederick had married Clara Lowenstein in Chicago in 1935, shortly after Clara's arrival in the United States, and had started a medical practice in Rochester. The son of a renowned medical professor from a

---

[221] Jenny last received word from Therese/Rose in 1937. A few postcards and letters survive; they are clearly self-censored. Therese writes of the family's pleasant apartment in Leningrad, of abundant food, and of the excellent medical education her son Emmanuel was receiving. Little of this is to be believed.

[222] Frederick was the father of this book's co-editor Olga Wise.

bustling German metropolis was now a Depression-era country doctor in the United States. Jenny rented rooms in a nearby home, and remained in Rochester until 1941.

Jenny moved in 1941 to the home of her nephew Erich Fraenkel (son of James and Paula Fraenkel) and wife Erna in Washington, D. C. In 1944 she came to Chicago and took up residence with Clara and her three children, the twins Olga and Philipp (born 1941) and their younger brother Fred (born 1943). The country was in the midst of war, and Frederick was serving as a U.S. Army physician in the Pacific Theater. Money was scarce and food was rationed. Under difficult circumstances, Clara headed a household whose members ranged in age from one to eighty-five. Frederick returned to Chicago in February 1946 to complete his residency in pathology. At the end of that year, the Bornstein family, including Jenny and new baby Aaron (born November 1946) moved to southern Illinois, where Frederick had found work as a pathologist in Herrin. Jenny lived in Herrin until her death in 1951.

❧ ❧

MY RECOLLECTIONS
OF JENNY

BY OLGA WISE

After we moved to Herrin, Illinois, I visited my great-grandmother Jenny often in the rooms she rented in a house a few blocks away from us (the landlady had a ferocious Spitz dog that barked furiously whenever I arrived). Jenny cut an unusual figure in her neighborhood; a diminutive lady just over five feet tall, she wore ankle-length dresses and walked with a fine wooden cane. Jenny loved reading the *Reader's Digest,* and would gleefully tell me the latest horror story revealed in its pages. I remember very clearly one article warning that hot dogs were made from horsemeat. Can that be why I have never liked hot dogs? I do not remember whether Jenny and I spoke in English or in German; I do know that I never tired of spending time with her. Because our own house was noisy and crowded, it was a treat for me to be alone with my great-grandmother and to have her full attention.

My favorite memory from my time with Jenny is that of watching her braid her waist-length hair. It was grey but still streaked occasionally with blond. She would brush her hair and braid it carefully down to its very ends, and then wind it around at the nape of her neck and secure the braid with long tortoiseshell hairpins. She saved the hair she combed out by winding it around her finger and then placing it in a small container. What on earth did she do with it? Perhaps in her childhood people saved their hair for pillows? I sat at Jenny's knee and listened to story after story, many of which I have forgotten. I specifically remember her telling me the story in which, as a child, she was banished from the table because she would have been the thirteenth guest. As I deciphered Jenny's handwriting and realized that I already knew this story, the shock of recognition literally gave me goose bumps. I can see now that Jenny did not easily forget or forgive childhood injuries.

I recall different versions of two of the stories that Jenny included in her memoir. Regarding Philipp, Jenny told me they first met each other at her father's store, and that it was her "beautiful blue eyes" that caused Philipp to fall in love with her and decide to marry her. About her parents' divorce, I recall Jenny telling me that Israel divorced Bella because she had been seen "talking to an officer" while they were on summer vacation at the sea shore. Prussian officers, it would seem, were not paragons of moral virtue.[223]

Jenny died in early 1951 at the age of ninety-one, far from the Berlin of her birth and childhood. Her strong spirit saw her through many disappointments, hardships and tragedies, including the death of two adult children and her exile from

---

[223] As a graduate student in German literature, I later found resonances of Jenny's own history and of the stories she told in Theodor Fontane's novels of nineteenth-century German bourgeois life. In her decision to abandon medicine, for example, Jenny called to mind Fontane's self-sacrificing heroines (*opferbereite Frauen*).

Germany. She accomplished much in her life. The family medical tradition she began was taken up by her son, grandson, and two of her four great-grandchildren. Her American descendants are now in their fourth generation.

ADDITIONAL PHOTOGRAPHS AND DOCUMENTS

Fig. 11. Gravestones of Israel and Therese Barth, Weissensee Cemetery, Berlin (German)

Fig. 12. Gravestones of Israel and Therese Barth, Weissensee
Cemetery, Berlin (Hebrew)

Fig. 13. Gravestone of Philipp Bornstein (1843–1891),
Weissensee Cemetery, Berlin

Fig. 14. Jenny's medical diploma, University of Zürich, 1898

Fig. 15 (facing page). Jenny and family members, 1915 or 1916. Jenny, seated at lower right; Hanne, seated second from left next to husband Wilhelm. Paula, standing at top right. To Jenny's right, grandson Frederick and son Arthur.

Fig. 16 (this page). Jenny in Palestine, 1935 or 1936

Fig. 17. Jenny at seventy-eight, in 1937

Fig. 18. Jenny, November 1943, with her great-grandchildren

Fig. 19. Jenny in Herrin, Illinois, around 1949, with grandson Frederick, his wife Clara, and great-grandchildren Aaron (on lap), Olga, Fred and Philipp (ascending order)

THE MEMOIR'S
TRANSLATORS/EDITORS

Olga and David Wise live in Austin, Texas. Olga holds B.A. and M.A. degrees in German from Washington University in St. Louis and a Master's Degree in Library and Information Science from the University of Illinois. She taught German at the college level and worked for many years as an information professional in academic and corporate libraries. David has a Ph.D. (Spanish and Portuguese) from the University of Illinois. He has worked as a college teacher, attorney, and professional translator.

BIBLIOGRAPHY

Bleker, Johanna and Sabine Schleiermacher. *Ärztinnen aus dem Kaiserreich: Lebensläufe einer Generation.* Weinheim: Deutscher Studien Verlag, 2000.

Bonner, Thomas N. "Pioneering in Women's Medical Education in the Swiss Universities 1864–1914." *Gesnerus (Swiss Journal for the History of Medicine and Sciences)*, Vol. 45 (1988).

Brinkschulte, Eva. *Weibliche Ärzte: die Durchsetzung des Berufsbildes in Deutschland.* Berlin, Edition Hentrich, 1993.

Dachs, Giesela, ed. *Frauen.* Berlin: Leo Baeck-Institut, 2006.

Efron, John M. *Medicine and the German Jews: A History.* New Haven: Yale University Press, 2001.

Elon, Amos. *The Pity of It All: A Portrait of the German Jewish Epoch, 1743–1933.* New York: Picador, 2002.

Faesecke, Karl-Peter. *Ein Pressluftartz für Hamburg: die medizinische Forschungsarbeiten von Arthur und Adele Bornstein beim Bau des ersten Hamburger Elbtunnels.* Kiel: Edition Trident, 1998.

Gay, Ruth. *The Jews of Germany: A Historical Portrait.* New Haven: Yale University Press, 1992.

Hertz, Deborah. *Jewish High Society in Old Regime Berlin.* New Haven: Yale University Press, 1988.

Hertz, Deborah. *How Jews Became Germans. The History of Conversion and Assimilation in Berlin.* New Haven: Yale University Press, 2007.

Kaplan, Marion, ed. *Jewish Daily Life in Germany 1618–1945.* New York: Oxford University Press, 2005.

Kaplan, Marion. *The Making of the Jewish Middle Class. Women, Family, and Identity in Imperial Germany.* New York: Oxford University Press, 1991.

Meyer, Paulette. "Women Doctors Refashion a Men's Profession: Medical Careers of Nineteenth-Century Zürich University Graduates in Germany." Ph.D. dissertation, University of Minnesota, 1997.

Richarz, Monika, ed. *Jewish Life in Germany: Memoirs from Three Centuries*. Bloomington: Indiana University Press, 1991.

Richarz, Monika, ed. *Jüdisches Leben in Deutschland*. Vol. 2, Selbstzeugnisse zur Sozialgeschichte im Kaiserreich. Stuttgart: Deutsche Verlags-Anhalt, 1979.

Stories of an Exhibition: Two Millennia of German Jewish History. Berlin: Jewish Museum Berlin, 2001.

Taylor, Ronald. *Berlin and Its Culture*. New Haven: Yale University Press, 1997.

Wegweiser durch das jüdische Berlin: Geschichte und Gegenwart. Berlin: Nicolai Verlag, 1987.

J. Barth

Berlin. Großbeeren Str. 1